13 Months

Diary of a Caregiver's Grief

Jaye Tee

91st and Hays Press

13 Months: Diary of a caregiver's Grief by Jaye Tee

Published in the United States of America by 91st and Hays Press.
© 2019 Jaye Tee

ISBN: 978-0-578-65082-1

All rights reserved. No part of this publication may be reproduced in whole or in part, or transmitted in any form or by any means, electronic, mechanical, photocopying, recording, or otherwise, without written permission of the publisher, except for the use of brief quotations for review purposes.

Interior design by Ferdinand Po

Cover by ebooklaunch.com

This is a work of creative nonfiction. The events are depicted to the best of the author's memory. While all the stories in this book are true, some names and identifying details have been changed to respect the privacy of the people involved.

In memory of Marty.
For teaching me that attitude is everything.

13 Months

Month 1

Everyone can master a grief but he that has it.

—William Shakespeare, *Much Ado About Nothing*

While I was growing up, my grandma seemed to possess magical skills that could comfort and uplift me in any situation. She would regularly swoop in and wave her magic wand when I was faced with even the illusion of catastrophe, to find and reveal the humor and the lessons in the most dismal of times.

One day, during my regular routine of sitting in front of the television, watching Mr. Rogers' Neighborhood, I could barely contain my excitement when I heard that he would be giving us a "behind the scenes" tour of The Neighborhood of Make-Believe. Mesmerized by what I believed to be a real neighborhood, it was always my favorite part of the show. I envisioned that one day, when I grew up, this would be where I would move to. My mind swirling in anticipation of the new things I might discover about my future neighborhood, I waited as patiently as I could for the start of the tour.

Sitting up straight and cross-legged in front of the TV, my excitement quickly turned to horror as I saw Mr. Rogers slowly unlock a storage case and take the puppets out one by one. As he brought each puppet to life using his hand and morphed his voice into each of the different characters, it swiftly descended on me what all this meant—that the Neighborhood of Make-Believe did not actually exist. With frantic breath, I squeezed my eyes shut and started waving my hands in front of the TV, desperately trying to wash away the reality of what was behind the curtain.

When Grandma told me her side of this story, she shared how she had first heard my short sobs coming from the living room and rushed in from the kitchen wondering what had happened. She said she'd found me curled over on my side, holding my head in both hands. When she propped me up, I quickly wrapped my arms around her and revealed my shock over what had unfolded right in front of my eyes. Grandma continued to hold and rock me as I shared my heartbreak over realizing that I would never be able to move to this neighborhood or live alongside King Friday and Henrietta Pussycat.

But the distress I find myself in now is no make-believe. My panic is real, and I honestly don't know what to do next. I want to appear normal. I want to order myself to figure out how to act appropriately in public.

But I don't feel normal.

My grandma has just died. After being her social companion and caregiver in one form or another for close to fifteen years, she is gone. These last two weeks, filled with so many twists and turns, have left me exhausted. I feel anesthetized. After numbly taking care of what hospice has requested, my friend Tara insists that I get something to eat. I agree to go with her to a café where we often meet after work. Being a warm and sunny morning, she suggests that we sit at one of the outside tables under the lush green trees.

"It'll be good for you to get some fresh air," she says.

As I walk with Tara, only confusion sets in. I can't walk normally. I bark at myself to slow down. This is Sunday. Every weekend she was with me. But with her age and frailness, she was unable to walk this fast. I feel like I am betraying her by walking at this pace.

My mind, trying to digest all that has happened, is playing tricks on me. It feels as if she is walking behind me trying to keep up. She is wearing one of her breezy, pastel, summer skirt and blouse outfits that she would always wear when I was young. This can't be, and I assume this is due to shock and lack of sleep.

Yet I can't help it. It's like she is right here, waving me down. Trying to catch up.

I try to hold back the tears that well up in my eyes. Just breathe normally, I instruct myself. But I can't. I stop walking. I imagine people looking at me wondering what is going on, and I am frantic to appear normal. I push myself to at least act like I know how to behave.

But I can't. I refuse to abandon the spirit of her that I feel is behind me. Because I know she would never have abandoned me.

Throughout my life, my grandparents and their simple but solid, cottage-style home remained my one true safe haven. Growing up in the Midwest during the 1970s and '80s, it was the place I spent the majority of my time. When I wasn't there, I constantly thought about when I could return. Amidst any chaos I experienced in life, being there had the lulling ability to make my worries disappear and allow me to sink into a sense of safety, love and a reliable routine. Even if it was only temporary.

Within their home, my grandma served as the central force of love, safety and joy, not just for me, but many other family members. Whenever I entered the house, she would be right there, holding open the front screen door with one hand, ready to pat me on the head with the other. "Come on in, honey," she would always say. Once inside, I naturally gravitated toward all that she lovingly offered and stayed firmly attached at her hip for most of my upbringing.

Long retired from her time working at local bakeries, while also being a homemaker and Sunday school teacher, Grandma often wore a homemade 1950s-style apron wrapped around her waist. I can still so clearly recall the way she used to push up her gold, wire-rimmed glasses, followed by a fleeting stroke to her short, auburn home-colored hair as if to make sure each curl was still in its place.

Although only five feet tall, her life presence was undeniable. Grandma was no pushover; she possessed this solid, strong force about her. Never self-conscious about her stature or sixth-grade education, she rarely hesitated in going toe to toe with any contender who tried to give her a hard time. Yet she also had a way of charming and finessing people. When she put this combination of traits to use, I witnessed even the hardest of personalities melt and give into what she was asking of them. Had she pursued it, I truly believe she could have been a very successful con artist.

I saw these character traits put to use in other ways. Easily riled up when someone was being bullied, excluded or abandoned, she often talked about the need to "stick up for the little guy." If she noticed that someone was being forgotten or ignored, she made a point of reaching out to them. Even during the times when she was rebuffed in her efforts, she continued to keep her heart open and welcoming, awaiting an opportunity to remind them that they were valued and wanted.

Knowing all of this about her, guilt rips me apart as I believe that walking too fast means abandoning and leaving her behind. Even as I doubt and question the reality of her presence, I can't deny what I feel. Yet I continue to pressure myself to look normal. Torn by two sides, I order myself to find a way to keep walking and not cry, biting the inside of my mouth to stop the tears.

Suddenly, Tara grabs my arm, her eyes gentle with understanding. "Let me help you," she says.

Hours later, sitting in the waiting area at the hospice office, I am finally able to behave in a way I consider normal. The first of my thirteen months of grief counseling is about to begin.

Trained as a therapist myself, I am familiar with the counseling process and have tried to prepare accordingly. While I now work in a different capacity and have not worked full-time as a therapist in a while, I still thought it wise to try designing a focused and productive start for these sessions—a general road map to follow.

Poised on my lap is a list. A list of everything I want to remind myself to be grateful for. This is how I have decided I should be grieving. Focus on the positive. Be thankful for all the time I had. Having established in advance the appropriate way to use these thirteen months of counseling, I am determined to govern this grief process with a stern hand.

When they call my name, an uncontrollable urge washes over me. One that I don't understand but can't resist. Something pushing me to take control of whatever I can. I get up and walk into the room, noticing a sofa next to the doorway and two chairs positioned on the far side. Feeling a need to stay close to the door, I sit on the sofa.

The urge grows, and I'm unable to refrain from taking charge of the session itself.

Diary of a Caregiver's Grief

"I have a list I want to go over," I blurt out.

My grief counselor glances down slightly in the direction of the piece of paper. She then looks back up at me, smiles warmly and asks with genuine curiosity, "What's on the list?"

Sensing sincerity and kindness in her voice, I'm put enough at ease to answer her question.

"Happy reminders of my grandma and my time with her," I say. "I want to use the list to keep my focus on the positive, to make sure I am remembering everything I have to be grateful for."

This is the right way to use these months of grief counseling, I think to myself. *Using the time to ingrain all that should be appreciated.* What I don't tell her is the why behind my plan: that I believe genuine grief would be too self-indulgent given the circumstance. Considering all the time I had with her, it would be selfish and weak of me to give in to my sadness. Grief is really for those who have tragically lost someone—and lost someone too soon.

Leaving this part out, I say, "What more could I have asked for? I had so much time with her. She gave me so much love, and I have so much to appreciate."

We go over the list, one item at a time and I prescribe how I can use each one in some way to create a positive focus moving forward.

"With this list, I think I now have a plan," I say emphatically once I've finished. "Plans are good."

Even on my way out of the office I can't stop dictating

to myself to focus on the positive, the list clenched in my fist. Stick to this plan and things will turn out okay, I keep repeating to myself.

In reality, I had no idea what grief had in store for me.

Month 2

The Mustard Seed

—Buddhist Parable

DURING THE BUDDHA'S TIME, there lived a woman named Kisa Gotami. She married young and gave birth to a son. One day, the baby fell sick and died soon after. Kisa Gotami loved her son greatly and refused to believe that he was dead. She carried the body of her son around her village, asking if there was anyone who could bring her precious boy back to life.

The villagers all saw that the child was clearly beyond saving. Nothing could be done. They advised her to accept his death and make arrangements for the funeral.

In terrible grief, she fell on her knees and clutched her son's lifeless body close to her body. She kept uttering, "Wake up, please wake up."

A village elder took pity on her and suggested she consult the Buddha.

"Kisa Gotami, we cannot help you. But perhaps he can bring your son back to life."

Kisa Gotami grew extremely excited upon hearing the elder's words. She immediately went to the Buddha's residence and pleaded for him to return her son to her.

"Kisa Gotami," said the Buddha, "I know of a way to bring your son back to life."

"My Lord, I will do anything."

"Then you must do one thing," the Buddha said. "You must bring me a mustard seed."

"Is that all?" Kisa Gotami could not believe her ears.

"Yes," the Buddha said. "But the mustard seed must come from a house where no one residing has ever lost a family member. Bring this seed back to me and your son will live once more."

Having great faith in the Buddha's promise, Kisa Gotami began her search. She went from house to house, trying to find the mustard seed.

At the first house, a young woman eagerly offered to give her some mustard seeds. But when Kisa Gotami asked if she had ever lost a family member to death, the young woman said her grandmother died a few months ago.

Kisa Gotami thanked the young woman and explained

why the mustard seeds did not fulfill the Buddha's requirements.

She moved on to the second house. There, a husband had died a few years before. The third house had lost an uncle, and the fourth house had lost an aunt. Kisa Gotami kept moving from house to house, but the answers were always the same—every house had lost a family member to death.

Kisa Gotami finally came to realize that there is no one in the world who had never lost a family member in this way. She understood that death was inevitable and a natural part of life.

Putting aside her grief, Kisa Gotami buried her son in the forest. She then returned to the Buddha and became his follower.

~~~

My body is standing among the crowd at the Saturday farmers' market, but my mind is lost among memories of my grandma from when I was a child.

One of our favorite activities was to take the bus somewhere and go out to lunch. But these were no regular lunches. Grandma would always insist on a fancy meal in an expensive restaurant with fine tablecloths and chic sounding entrees on the menu. Elegant desserts like Baked Alaska or Bananas Foster whirled in front of us at the end of the meal.

However, after lunch was finished, there were strict instructions to follow. She would go over them with me every time and make me repeat them back to her on the bus ride home. She would hold my hand firmly and say, "Remember, when Grandpa asks, we say we only had a couple of cheese sandwiches. Got it, honey?"

Being on a strict budget, my grandpa would have bellowed, hands thrown up in the air in disbelief, over what was really going on in these outings. My grandma had to skillfully devise and concoct both the adventures and the subsequent cover-ups to carefully avoid any suspicion. Sometime after we got home, my grandpa would inevitably ask about the lunch. Usually, I was in the back bedroom playing, but I could always hear Grandma's effortless response.

"Just a couple of cheese sandwiches, that's all."

Satisfied with this response, my grandpa never suspected a thing.

I am recalling this now because it feels as though I am following in her footsteps somehow, creating my own cover-up. What exactly I'm covering up, I don't know.

After concocting what I believe to be a fool-proof plan to stay positive and control how my grief process will unfold throughout the remainder of my thirteen months of counseling, I burst out of the gate in a frenzy to put it into action. I am driven by a desperate urgency to take charge and find a way to direct grief's storyline. Petrified that if I don't establish this dominance from the start, I will get swallowed up by the looming, terrifying presence of grief, lagging only steps behind me, breathing down my neck as if it were the

Big Bad Wolf to my Little Red Riding Hood. Certain that grief will engulf me if I don't keep moving, I take the first of many steps in creating a scenario in which grief and I are starkly at odds. Like I'm running a race against grief, and I need to sprint as fast as I can.

Structure emerges as the first target in my plan. Structure, I start by telling myself. You need to develop some structure. Without the routine and schedule I had while my grandma was alive, I need to create something new. I know this because I can't stop checking my phone for missed calls and messages, a gnawing worry telling me Grandma needs something. But no one has called and there are no messages to hear. When I look at my schedule, I know nothing is really there as everything has been cancelled. In spite of this, I can't bring myself to delete the contacts, tasks and appointments still listed. Even thinking about getting rid of all this unsettles me. It has been a long time since my life wasn't planned and scheduled around my grandma, in one way or another.

The schedule first began with a frequent number of social visits shortly after my grandpa died. I began coming around to spend time with Grandma to keep her company. This period happened to coincide with my time in graduate school for counseling, and I was in her city on a regular basis. Still, my visits were initially sporadic as my grandma continued to be very active socially. Between visits with other family members and a multitude of church events and senior trips, Grandma delighted in the fullness of life. Since she often had other things planned, on several occasions, she didn't need me to come over. Even so, it always warmed my heart to look over the paper calendar she kept atop her rolltop desk in the corner of the living room, where, scrawled out in cursive for my weekends with her, she would write: *Jaye visits*.

Over the next seven years, my visits gradually shifted to meet her changing needs. I settled into a more regular routine of coming every other weekend, and the schedule became more specific.

Friday I would arrive with a fish fry in hand for dinner. We would sit at the dining room table, and she would share stories from her week and ideas about what she wanted to do that weekend.

Saturday was always her standing appointment at the hairdresser. While she was there, I would go to the grocery store with a list of whatever she needed. After shopping and putting the groceries away, I would pick her up and we would go to lunch. On our way back, we could hardly ever resist the Krispy Kreme drive-through, especially when the "Hot Donuts Now!" sign was blazing. I rarely managed to get the box into the car before Grandma was reaching over my arm trying to tear into it, even though home was only five minutes away. Back at the house, we would settle in to rest and get ready for *Lawrence Welk*. She knew most of the songs by heart and would rock back and forth in her chair, belting them as if she were part of the chorus. She adored every single show, even after seeing them countless times before.

Sunday was always for church.

We kept up the routine for quite a while until something unexpected occurred. Arriving on a Friday evening, I walked in to find her looking out the window as she pushed the curtain aside with the back of her hand. She was clearly annoyed.

"Is everything okay, Grandma?" I asked, knowing something wasn't right.

Still staring out the window, she unleashed the contents of her mind. "Well, just look at them!" she exclaimed. "What do they think they're doing holding a carnival out in the back yard? I was just about to go out there and tell them they have to leave, because where would you park your car?"

Glancing out the partially opened window to where she was pointing, I could see nothing of what she described. All I saw was the same old back yard with its lilac tree starting to blossom and the unused garage. Never having experienced anything like this with her before, I froze. I couldn't think of a single thing to say. Finally, I attempted at least to reassure her.

"Well, I was able to park my car just fine so I think things are okay."

Suddenly remembering the fish dinner I was still holding in my hand, I added, "I have your Friday fish fry, Grandma. Would you like me to set it up before it gets too cold? We can talk more about what's going on while we eat and figure out if there is something I can do."

This seemed to adjust her focus. She eagerly sat down

with me at the dining room table. As we ate, I learned more about what she was seeing. She told me that a small children's carnival had stationed itself outside during the day. She didn't like their games and she was annoyed by the rides taking up space in the driveway.

While listening and trying to soothe her, I couldn't stop thinking of one thing. I needed to talk to my grandma's younger sister, Millie, as soon as possible. During those years, Millie served as Grandma's central companion. Since Grandma was stable and active, we did not have to collaborate too much. We just knew that we were both involved in keeping her company and in arranging tasks that needed to be done. That was all about to change for both of us.

The next day, while my grandma was at the hairdresser, I called Millie and told her everything that had happened. Concerned and unsure, she agreed to make an appointment at the doctor as soon as possible. We decided it would be better for Grandma not to be left alone and arranged for Millie to arrive at her house before I left.

From there I returned home several hours later and waited to hear from her. After the appointment, she called to share more details.

"He thinks it's from her macular degeneration," Millie explained.

Grandma had been diagnosed with this several years ago, when her eyesight had started to deteriorate. But until now, it had only impacted her reading. From this event, we learned about an added condition called Charles Bonnet

Syndrome which can cause people to see things that aren't really there.

"But she's okay, though?" I asked.

I heard a deep breath and then her voice say, "Yes, I think so. From what the doctor said these are normal issues with her age and memory. But she is okay and we can keep doing what we are doing for her with one change. He recommended that we increase our visits going forward so that we can monitor her more."

Millie and I took the doctor's recommendation and worked out a new schedule. We felt it would be better to create something more regular, so we decided to organize weekly care. However, Grandma was still fiercely independent and often didn't want certain types of help.

"I am going to live to be 100 years old," she regularly informed us, "and someone will have to drag me from this house, because I am not leaving!"

So, out of respect, we tried to plan cautiously. This new schedule seemed to be just what was needed, consisting of weekly coordination and check-ins, as well as actually handing off care to each other. With the new plan in place, once again, everything settled back into a routine. So much so that we believed what we had just gone through would be the worst of anything that could happen. Little did we know how wrong we would be.

All of this explains why the most obvious gap in my routine right now, is routine itself. Without it, I am confronted with an uncomfortable, gaping void of silence. While I still have my work schedule, there remains a glaringly large amount of empty time just hanging there. It's as if I am floating in limbo without the structure, planning and routine I had become accustomed to over the years.

To deal with this, I first tried to think about what I could do to create structure in order to keep my mind busy and positive. I zeroed in on the Saturday farmers' market knowing that the weekends will be the hardest. *Great choice*, I think! But when I am actually here, I robotically move around the market feeling nothing. Do I even like being here? The immediate internal response is that it doesn't matter. Just keep doing this. You will get the hang of it.

I do keep doing it, but nothing really changes. Each Saturday starts to take on the feel of a pre-assigned task I am coercing myself into doing rather than something I truly enjoy. Is this how it's supposed to be? Trying to conform to what I think I should be doing?

Then, one Saturday, something happens. In the midst of a number of food carts, a bright pink and orange cart with banners flying high catches my attention. When I get closer, the name on the food cart is clear to see: Sweet Fried Delights. Curious, I want to step up close but there is a line. So, I wait until I can get closer to read the menu. And when I finally do, I feel a rush of glee come over me as I read that some of the items offered include deep-fried cookie dough balls and deep-fried ice cream sandwiches. I decide to try the cookie dough balls first and find a spot to sit outside of the market traffic. Biting into one, I feel a spark of joy. As I continue eating, powdered sugar covers my face and the joy stays. Not forced, but real joy.

This encounter causes me to quickly veer off course. After sinking my teeth into that all too gooey and sugary goodness, I am hooked. Each Saturday I now use going to the market as a cover story for my true destination of the Sweet Fried Delights food cart. I am clearly aware that coming here *does* actually make me happy; I just can't allow myself to accept that as it doesn't fit into the idea of my original plan. It's definitely not healthy to be eating like this on a regular basis and it doesn't match up with the idea of a productive and positive plan. Additionally, I'm actually embarrassed to admit that this is what I'm really doing every Saturday. I seriously doubt that I would find eating large quantities of deep-fried sugary dough at 10 a.m. on any list of self-care ideas for grieving caregivers. I don't think anyone would consider it to be a constructive goal. So, I mostly keep it as a secret to myself and continue the cover-up, ready to deliver a preplanned answer to anyone who asks. Just as my grandma did with my grandpa to conceal our decadent lunch outings.

And yet, my charade of going to the market first with Sweet Fried Delights as my last stop seems to be one of the only things that I really let myself enjoy. Outside of these rogue expeditions, I start keeping a list of structured activities that I think will keep my mind focused on something positive and constructive. Read affirmations every morning! Organize the kitchen! Eat more kale! Breathe and stay in the moment! Striving to comply with what I think I should be doing as I grieve, I direct myself not to spend too much time thinking about whether I actually enjoy any of them or not. Just keep at it.

But underneath, cracks in my plan to stay positive are already beginning to form.

Caregiving was not just something that I did; it was who I was. Over the years, it became a substantial part of my identity. Now, I don't really know who I am without it. Most people viewed me as part of a witty duo. Between the challenges and crises, there were always humorous tales to tell, like the time we were at the public botanical gardens. In her wheelchair, Grandma was close enough to a small pasture of flowers to bend forward toward them. I mistakenly thought this was an attempt to smell one of them, and, after turning my head to look at another area of the garden, I discovered that she had yanked out one of the rare blooms by its root. She saw the bewilderment in my eyes and simply said, "It was just sitting there, and I wanted it."

Or times when she would unabashedly put her feisty, vivacious and mischievous personality on display. Soon after moving her nearer to me, I found that Grandma never hesitated in cutting straight to the point to let me know what she thought or needed. One time, in a rush to pick her up, I left the house without combing my hair. Upon seeing me, she gasped. "You look like a flamingo!" she said.

Entering the care facility one weekend, I was greeted with sounds of an old gangster movie playing on TV. Spotting me soon after I came through the front door, Grandma belted out in a James Cagney voice, "Gee, kid, where've you been? We gotta get outta here; they're closing down the joint!"

Another time while doing her laundry, I curiously discovered several packets of sugar in her pockets. When I asked her about this, her matter-of-fact reply was that the oatmeal at the care facility was never sweet enough and that she had to "take matters into her own hands." I tried to figure out where she was getting these packets of sugar to begin with, and what else she might be "taking into her own hands," but my questions were met with complete silence. She refused to give up any further information.

Now there will be no new tales to tell when someone asks me what I did over the weekend.

And I'm starting to notice more and more sadness. I feel lost without her. In certain moments grief hits me so hard I can't breathe. Clinging even tighter to the belief that I should be grateful and positive, I try to whip myself back into shape by pushing away the "bad" grief.

Other, larger cracks arrive only at night. I begin to have nightmares. The theme is always the same. My grandma is in some type of distress. I can't reach her or find her. Something is always terribly wrong, and I am powerless to help her. I wake up, but the thoughts don't stop.

In an effort to keep my self-prescribed and predetermined plan on course, I go into my session this month wanting to talk about all the above. After gently listening to my descriptions, my grief counselor brings my attention to the metaphor of grief like ocean waves. She explains how the waves of grief can sometimes be as small as subtle ripples in the water. Other times, vast, overpowering waves will come out of nowhere to knock me over or pull me under.

I faintly hear her say that these waves may come and go. Part of me knows this is important to talk about, but another part drowns out her voice. I stare off into the corner of the room, not knowing what to say.

Month 3

Some people say that the weary blues ain't bad
Some people say the weary blues ain't bad
But it's the worst old feeling that I've ever had.

—Bessie Smith, "Mama's Got the Blues"

Between stifled sobs, I am able to get the words out.

"But I am ready now."

I am with my grief counselor detailing what has been happening. Even with the infrequent nightmares, I recognize that I am physically better. I'm more alert and well-rested than I have been in a long time. No longer sleep deprived from caregiving, I feel as if I have finally awakened from a hazy stupor. And now I am back and fully ready to return to caregiving.

But she's gone.

I try to explain as my grief counselor listens closely.

"It's just that, I've had a chance to rest, get back to my full strength, and now all I want to do to is plan things for us to do. I'm ready," I say. "I have so many ideas of new things to try."

I just can't comprehend that it's not going to happen.

This leads to ruminating on ways I let my grandma down. "Why did I have to get tired?" I ask Tara.

She looks at me, bewildered, unable to take in what I am saying. "Wait," she asks, "you mean you don't think you did enough? You have got to be kidding me," she adds. "You gave your grandma the five-star treatment at all times."

But I don't believe her; I can't believe her. All I can concentrate on and remember are the errors, lapses and oversights I am certain that I made.

And when I am alone, these thoughts begin to pile up and rotate through my mind.

How could I have forgotten the Depends?

Why didn't I pick up on her difficulty with swallowing earlier?

How could I have not foreseen that the bed alarm would become detached?

Why didn't I think to get a wheelchair sooner?

These particular questions stem from the time after Millie and I transitioned Grandma to be under my direct care. Before the transition, we continued with the arrangement of weekend visits for some time, but minor disruptions to the plan slowly started to surface. Something as simple as a schedule change. So easy to remedy that we never saw them as early warning signs.

More serious complications soon emerged. One after another, popping up out of nowhere and catching us both off-guard. A leak in the basement, the furnace going out and the roof needing repair. Grandma calling Millie to report ants crawling all over the living room carpet, only for Millie to rush over and find no ants in sight.

One weekend I found Grandma fretting over a bill she received for "special" envelopes. She told me how she agreed to purchase them from "such a nice sounding man" over the phone, and I realized she was a victim of a scam targeting the elderly. It took several days to report it and find out what steps were needed to remedy it and protect her.

Soon, it became harder and harder to deny the obvious: Our plan was no longer working. But neither of us was ready to face this, so we just kept pushing ahead, trying to make it work.

Then, another unexpected turn. This was the event that would forever change things. One Sunday, while getting ready for church, I noticed my grandma sitting on the edge of the bed wearing a look of clear confusion. Something was very wrong. I immediately called Millie, who instructed me to call the doctor's office. After detailing what had happened and answering a series of the doctor's questions, I was instructed to take her to the ER.

I called Millie back with an update. "We'll be leaving as

soon as I can finish dressing her."

"I'll meet you there," she replied.

Once we got Grandma admitted, we waited. And waited. After a long series of various tests, it was determined that my grandma had suffered a mini-stroke—what is commonly called a TIA—resulting in escalated dementia symptoms. They would be keeping her overnight, and we were told she could not live alone after this. As we tried to digest the new information and grapple with the next steps, we knew the trickiest part would be figuring out how to talk to Grandma about it.

"This is going to be hard for her," I whispered, staring down at the hospital floor.

"She's not going to like this news, is she?" Millie replied.

We sat next to each other, in silence, trying to come to grips with everything that was happening.

So, the plan changed once again, and we remained adamant we would make this new one work. Millie offered to have Grandma move in with her and to take over all her regular care. Grandma approved of this idea and we all agreed it was the best solution.

Now my weekend visits were about more than spending time with my grandma and offering general support. Being able to pick Grandma up from Millie's and take her back to "her little house" for a couple of days seemed to help her adjust better to the transition. The new routine also allowed me to support Millie, providing her with some much-needed time for herself and her family.

But the plan we hoped would solve everything turned out to be nothing but a Band-Aid fix. More issues erupted all the time, and the growing list of daily needs were beginning to take a toll.

Then, Grandma had a fall. This resulted in another hospital stay followed by a short-term stay in a rehabilitation facility. It was a whole new experience for both of us. As the hospital staff walked us through the type of care my grandma would need moving forward, we realized this would be no easy transition to manage.

With limited finances, my grandma only qualified for what could be called "sketchy options." These were places known for accidents, violations and short-staffing. It soon became distressingly clear that any idea of being through the worst was far from reality.

It also became obvious to both of us that, moving forward, caring for my grandma would now be too much for Millie. We could no longer stay in denial about this. After an honest discussion, we knew we had to, once again, come up with a new plan—a long-term care plan. But this time, we had no idea what it would be.

At first, we tried to explore the option of her staying in the facility where she was receiving rehab. Maybe it would be possible to transition her from that unit to the nursing unit? Only, when talking to the staff about the process, red flags immediately emerged. We were met with questions and phrases such as "Are you sure you don't have other options?" or "Let's see if there is a way to extend her time in rehab."

When I visited, it was standard to hear yelling and screaming throughout the halls, accompanied by the stench of vomit and urine. Even more disturbing was the sight of coroner staff in the hallway—wheeling someone out right in front of everyone.

Most heart-wrenching was the level of distress and agitation my grandma demonstrated during her time at the rehab facility. This escalated with an incident where they found my grandma on the floor with indications that the other person in her room had pushed her. The staff did all they could to move her to a safer space, but even then things were not good. When it came time for any of the family to say goodbye, she would usually burst into tears.

One thing became very clear. We needed to get her out of there.

The only option I could think of was to move her nearer to me so that I could take over her care. After talking with several resources in senior care options and focusing on what would provide the greatest safety and quality of life for my grandma, I was convinced this would be the best decision. I was also convinced I was up to the task.

Agreeing to the plan, Millie worked with me to figure out how to manage the move, what the new routine would be and how to talk with my grandma about it. Due to my work schedule, we agreed she would need to stay at a memory care facility during most of the week, but she would spend every weekend with me. I would pick her up on Fridays and return her on Monday mornings. I was nervous about how

Grandma might respond to this new proposal, but I was also elated to get her out of there. So much so, that the next time I saw her I was unable to contain my excitement and cut straight to the point.

"Grandma, I am busting you out of here," I said.

"Really, you mean it?" she asked with widening eyes.

I sat down beside her to reveal all the details and then asked if she thought she might like to give this plan a try.

"You bet I would!" she said.

But as honestly excited as I was about having this time with her, I was also incredibly naive about the realities of this level of caregiving.

At first, Grandma seemed to settle in seamlessly. She would often remark how happy she was and how she liked all the activities I had been able to find for us to do. The staff at the care facility where she stayed during the week regularly commented to me how much fun she was and how so many people delighted in talking with her.

Her sparkling wit drew the most attention. She regularly wowed and made people laugh with her clever responses. Several staff, Jenna, Neecy and Sandy, always updated me on her banter and I would, in turn, share many of her quotes. In particular, she showed a fondness for declaring herself "Madam Lasagna" and, if I was coming to pick her up tomorrow and not today as she wanted, would proclaim:

"Tomorrow, tomorrow—it's always tomorrow!" During craft time she was known to raise her hand and exclaim, "I could use a little glitter over here."

Once the transition was complete, there still remained so much to do, and it began to quickly sink in that there was never enough time to get everything done. I erroneously thought that things would be easier to manage since she was now with me. However, this was far from the reality. In addition to every weekend with me, I also tried to call or stop in at the facility during the week whenever I could. Multiple doctor's appointments, responding to phone calls (often in the middle of the night), errands and tasks related to her care filled each week. Also to contend with were the episodes, crises and hospitalizations that popped up unexpectedly. Yet I knew that my situation was nothing special, and these events were standard for any caregiver to experience. So I tried my best to attend to these needs and everything else while also maintaining my regular work schedule. But no matter how many scheduling strategies and tricks I tried, I could never keep up. Each week, I was lagging further and further behind with the tasks that needed to be done. More and more, I began to feel as if I had fallen into what can only be described as a pit of caregiver quicksand and, as I sank, I berated myself about what I had forgotten or what I should have thought of sooner.

Even though reminders of these past concerns have no purpose now, I am unwilling to let them go.

Also creeping in are doubts. Skepticism of whether I was

ever a "real" caregiver. Did I really do that much? Other people do so much more, I say over and over to myself. Also, I had help. My partner Alejandro and several friends provided indispensable support, often on a moment's notice. I would have been lost without them. So many other caregivers don't have any help so I have no right to claim that I was a "real" caregiver.

Taunting and chastising me, these revolving doubts and questions begin to escalate in my mind. The ways I let my grandma down. What I forgot or didn't remember soon enough while she was under my care. My "legitimacy" of being a caregiver. Like an invasive plant species, they quickly spread until they consume every corner of my mind, leaving no room for any type of positive thought from my plan to find a way to enter.

In this race, grief has now officially taken the lead.

Month 4

I can't go back to yesterday because I was a different person then.

—Lewis Carroll, *Alice in Wonderland*

I DON'T REALIZE IT YET, but I am pulling myself in multiple directions. Emotionally, I am so all over the place that I don't recognize myself anymore. I thought at some point I would go back to who I was, to a time before the caregiving and grief. But that doesn't seem to be happening. I know this because almost none of my old habits spark any joy or interest. I once thoroughly enjoyed traveling to Mexico and Texas. Or baking and cooking for friends and family. But that person went away and hasn't returned. I am left with what feels like a foreign entity in control of my mind and body.

This new person spends hours disinterestedly watching National Geographic's *The '80s* in the dark because it seems like too much trouble to get up and turn on a light or reach for the remote. My eating habits have taken more peculiar turns. In addition to the sugar sprees, I have now developed a compulsion to devour cheeseburgers. A lot of them. All of the time. And always using the drive-through because the idea of actually getting in and out of the car twice in one go seems like a Herculean task.

Amidst these new, unwanted, quirky habits, I notice that I can't seem to get my energy back, and I find myself getting anxious over nothing. All I want to do is stay home. None of this feels familiar or comfortable. The only exception to this, the one time when I feel a spark or glimmer of my old self, is when I hear a specific set of four words: The San Antonio Spurs.

My love and rabid support of this basketball team came on very unexpectedly, all thanks to my partner, Alejandro. When we first started dating, we made attempts to discover interest in things the other enjoyed. For Alejandro, it was immediately clear to me that basketball and the San Antonio Spurs were a big deal. When we met, I knew virtually nothing about the game. I doubt I would have had a chance picking a basketball out of a lineup featuring balls from every professional sport. I knew nothing at all about the rules. At all. So, I tried to learn, and Alejandro tried to be patient, but this was one steep learning curve. While watching one of my first games, I asked why they kept stopping and interrupting just for one player to shoot the ball. Before answering, Alejandro cocked his head a little, trying to determine if I was, in fact, being serious.

Determining I was, he quietly answered. "Because there was a foul and this is a free throw."

Or the time I asked if we were done with the second session. Again, looking at me curiously until he figured out what I meant, he responded. "They're called periods. And yes, the second period is over. It's now half-time."

But then something unforeseen happened. I started to enjoy watching the Spurs play. A lot. So much so that one night, at the end of my waitressing shift, I went into the empty bar area and asked if one of the TVs could be turned to ESPN.

Several of my co-workers were standing nearby. "Are you joking?" someone asked.

Still looking up at the TV, I said, "I want to see if the Spurs won. It's the playoffs, you know."

All at once, my co-workers burst out laughing. "I can't believe this," one of them said. "If you had asked Jaye five months ago what color a basketball was, she probably would have said blue or purple."

Things continued from there until, during the next season, Alejandro started to wonder if he had created a monster. I had lost the ability to sit still during a game. I would regularly jump up, pull my hair and shout about how the Spurs needed to dominate the low post.

So, now, at my low point, the Spurs seem to be the one thing that can jolt me back into feeling more normal. But since the season is over, all I am left with are games on the DVR and, even of those, I am selective in which I want to watch. Needing to control the outcome, I only rewatch the games where the Spurs triumphed. I make the insistent proclamation to Alejandro that he is not to delete any of these games from the DVR. Ever.

He looks at me like I am out of my mind. "Jaye," he says, "that's an awful lot of space. There are other ways to watch or keep these. We have . . ."

He stops, noticing me shaking my head. A little exasperated, he pleads with me to realize technology has advanced quite a lot. There are other ways to maintain this collection. But I want to watch them just like this: in the dark, my preferred ambience of the moment. We go around and around until, finally, we reach a truce. Alejandro agrees to leave them for now, and I agree to make puffy tacos on a more frequent basis.

But this bounce back is a rare exception. Most of the time, I don't know who I am anymore, plagued by the question of why it is taking so long to get back to my "normal" self. One thing's for sure, and that is the more I pull myself in different directions, the further I drift from who I remember myself to be.

In one direction, my plan to stay positive reminds me

that there is nothing special about me or my situation. Everyone loses someone they love. Everyone deals with loss and death. Everything I'm experiencing is a natural part of life and, even more, so many others have had time with their loved ones cut very, very short. My beneficial circumstance of having had so much time with my grandma is not lost on me. I do not believe my attitude is bad in and of itself. It's just that I force myself to do it even when any feeling of sadness and grief wants to surface. Whenever they arise, I pounce quickly, desperate to wipe them out as soon as I can. During times when I believe I am feeling "too" sad (sadder than I should be), I push myself to try and get rid of all grief, change the storyline and find a way to replace it with something more favorable, more "cheery." At this point, I associate any and all feelings related to grief as the enemy. The only purpose grief seems to serve is as a stubborn obstruction against my plan to stay positive. Not something to accept or tolerate, I view it as something to annihilate and eliminate as quickly as possible.

This does work for a while, but it also generates internal confusion. Is what I am thinking true? Is it really a good idea to jump over any and all grief and sadness? Dive straight to where I feel resilience and triumph? But if I don't, am I just being weak? Wouldn't everyone prefer to jump to the part of their story where all the obstacles are overcome? And what would be the ultimate cost of such a plan?

Brewing under the surface is another motive for jumping to the positive: *Other people prefer it.* I am at the point in this process where I notice my feelings and grief make many others uncomfortable. Then there are those who I can tell are clearly anxious for me to reach the story's victorious, happy ending, where I have overcome all of grief's hurdles. I can detect when people avoid eye contact or develop a distracted, slightly glazed look to my honest responses when they ask how I am doing. There is often a syncopated release of *hmm* and *uh-huhs* instead of any engaged response. Even though these reactions generate more pain and shame for me, I can understand them. For many of us, it can be very uncomfortable to softheartedly listen to the part of the story where someone continues to express pain and suffering after we have determined that the appropriate amount of time has expired. When grief and pain linger, few are willing to patiently sit with you in that. In these moments, all I feel is shame for my prolonged, drawn out grieving.

But shame is no stranger. It has made its presence known many other times in my life. During times of real tragedy, my grandma had regularly rushed in when she sensed that shame was engulfing me. Times when I was unable to get out of bed due to depression and anxiety or in a state where I revisited distressing events in my mind over and over again, constantly questioning if there was something, anything, I could have and should have done to prevent the domestic violence or abuse. Shame was always there, ready to descend and consume me. But my grandma would not have it. Fueled by her unwavering faith in being compassionate and comforting to someone when they were suffering, her healing presence and firm, strong voice offered me a life raft from shame.

One day, while sitting on the edge of the bed with me while wearing one of her dainty skirt and sweater combinations, she raised her hand as if to emphatically underline what she was telling me.

"No, honey, what you are thinking about yourself just isn't true. Things like this should never happen to you or anyone else. Just turn to the Lord and listen for how to move forward, not backward."

As if knowing that my inner voice continued to plague me with criticism and self-doubt, she instinctively reached for my hand and said, "I will always believe in you. I know that Jesus is here to help you overcome this."

She always listened and tried to understand, while never judging or belittling me. She inspired me to believe I had the ability to overcome anything and to move forward. Her words alone would often be enough to help keep shame at bay.

Now shame is back again, with a vengeance. Just as before, I always feel shame first. Before I am conscious of its presence and can verbally call it out. I know it's there when I first have the feeling of something blocking my throat, trapping my voice and preventing me from finding the words to respond to the person who is shaming me. An icky, oozing sensation slowly creeps over my body, telling me I am worthless until all I want to do is curl up into a ball and disappear.

Occasionally, after shame has run its course, rage flares up. Like an animal trapped in a corner, I want to strike back and be shaming and demeaning in return, but when I do, it always backfires. The result is deep remorse, and I become more rageful and shaming toward myself—feeling worse and pushing people further away in the process.

I know that I want out of this cycle, but I don't know the way. Instead, I settle on trying to look deeper and consider what others might be feeling. *Am I really trying to understand someone else? Am I being fair here?* When I ask myself these questions, I know I am not.

Recognizing this, I become pulled in another direction. The discomfort and desire to fast-forward the grief process that I detect from others seems to get at the heart of something bigger, something I don't think I am alone in wanting to avoid: vulnerability. Feeling my own or witnessing someone else's has usually brought on fear and panic. I think all of us end up in both spots eventually, usually multiple times, throughout life. Neither feels good and one can easily spill over like water into the other.

When feeling vulnerable, I have always found it hard to ask for support, wondering what others will think of me and not liking the feeling of losing control. Grandma once put it this way: "When you get old and can't do things for yourself anymore, sometimes people want to rush in and do everything for you. It's not as great as it sounds." The other side, witnessing vulnerability, has often made me feel like I don't know what to say or do. In the past, when I have been in this spot, it was often accompanied with ripple thoughts going back to my own most powerless moments. Grief, pain, vulnerability and fear. Isn't it all just messy, scary stuff for most of us?

My own heart softens when I am able to remember this instead of focusing on a tidy but usually incomplete view on how others are responding to me. Toward my grief, toward myself, toward those who can't tolerate me right now and, hopefully, toward everyone. Because we all seem to be running from the same thing.

This registers only briefly until I come back to the seductive idea of jumping over all this grief. Yes, this feels like the direction I want to bet on. Because everyone, including myself, is eager for a quick and happy ending. However, there's something else belligerently standing in my way, rooted in the fact that my grief does not like to be ignored.

As much as I might try to be positive and push any grief down, my real feelings are still there. And almost like the relief I feel when I can go home at the end of the day and change into sweatpants, is the relief I feel when I can be honest with someone about how I am really doing.

I am extremely grateful for the chance to be real with my pastor about the pressure to conceal my grief. I don't have to put on pretenses or sugarcoat anything with her. Pastor C reminds me that, even with a planned, expected loss, one's heart doesn't ache any less. I come back to this thought many times in private to remind myself that it is acceptable to feel my loss even when I also understand everything I am grateful for. The two are not mutually exclusive.

In the following weeks, Pastor C's open acceptance of my feelings and the guidance she offered seem to generate a lull in the intensity of my grief. I even notice that on occasion I am actually feeling joyful. During this time, I have a doctor's appointment for my annual exam, and I update her on my loss. When she asks how I'm doing, I am honest about my struggles and recount some of my more difficult days.

Then, still filled with optimism, I say, "Things really have felt more hopeful and encouraging these last weeks."

My doctor voices support and brings up additional treatments she can recommend if I need them. Going through each one, we talk the most about the benefits acupuncture has brought me in the past, along with different medications that can be beneficial during the grieving process. Understanding that all of her recommendations have the potential to help, I let her know I am open to considering any of them.

"It's just that, with things feeling better, I don't think I really need any additions right now."

We agree that I will keep her updated if I want to pursue any of these options in the future.

At the session with my grief counselor near the end of the month, my feelings change once again. I immediately dive in and ask how long it is "normal" to grieve.

"There is no timeline here," she stresses. "Everyone is different, and you need to take your time."

Diary of a Caregiver's Grief

I try to let that sink in, but then I have a knee-jerk reaction. "I didn't expect this to be so difficult and take so long," I suddenly blurt out. "I'm trained as a therapist for goodness sake! While I know that doesn't make me exempt from grief, I just thought I would be able to handle it better. But I am not handling this well at all. It just makes me feel like even more of a failure with everything."

After listening closely, she pauses and then tries to reassure me that it is okay for me to be feeling whatever it is I am feeling.

"It doesn't matter what training you have," she answers firmly. "You are still human. Grief is a human experience. Regardless of what someone does, everyone gets permission to feel what they need to feel. There is no supposed to, should do or expected to do with the grief process."

I try to focus on what she is saying, but my train of thought switches again and I jump to sharing my dismay at the outside pressure I feel to "get on with things." With more care and compassion, she urges me to just let myself be and allow these contrasting thoughts, feelings and waves of grief to come and go as they need. I nod my head and, once again, try to go back in the direction of being more respectful and understanding toward myself and this grief.

But this doesn't last either. Shortly after, yanked back in the other direction toward impatience and a desire to avoid any more pressure and shame, I walk out of her office holding tightly and quietly to what I really want to say to grief: *Hurry up and let's get this over and done with.*

Month 5

How often have I said to you that when you
have eliminated the impossible, whatever remains,
however improbable, must be the truth?

—Sir Arthur Conan Doyle, *The Sign of Four*

"Some people have these experiences, but not everyone."

I listen attentively to my grief counselor's explanation. I came into my session this month needing to talk about something new. While the waves of grief and different emotional struggles still persist, something else has moved to the forefront. I keep hearing my grandma's voice. Her real voice, telling me things. And I can feel her strong presence. Not every day and not with long phrases or conversations. But she is here. Unlike the nightmares, these unexpected encounters are usually whimsical and often sweet. At first, I thought it was just memories or crisp reminders of conversations we had. I have tried to dismiss it, eliminate what seemed impossible. But no, she really is here.

One morning, while eating breakfast at Espuma, I am unable to ignore it anymore. This was the café my grandma and I went to every week for breakfast. She always ordered the same thing and could never get enough of the chicken sausages included in the breakfast platter. She loved them so much that I once received a call at work from the care facility. Over the phone, one of the CNAs, Jenna, shared her confusion.

"She keeps asking for the sausages. Do you know what she means?"

I could tell right away what she meant. Laughing a little, I explained it to Jenna.

"Just tell her that we will definitely go for sausages when I pick her up next time."

"Why are there no sausages on the plate?" she asks.

It's clearly her voice. Looking down at what I ordered, all I see is an omelet and toast. No sausages. Not quite sure what to make of it all, I take a quick glance over my shoulder to check if anyone heard it too. Everyone else seems unfazed and busy with their own business, so I turn to look out the window.

So now what? Do I respond to her? Do I just ignore it? How can this be real? Can I just respond to her in my head and keep the whole thing secret? While confused, skeptical and unsure of what is happening exactly, I definitely don't want to give her the impression that I am ignoring her either. But I don't feel comfortable enough to just blurt out an answer in public. There is no way I am going to do that. She asks again. "How about those sausages?"

I take another glance around the room, wanting to be inconspicuous and keep everything that is happening under wraps as I decide what to do. No one seems to be noticing anything, but I am definitely becoming more anxious. I feel compelled to answer her in some way. So I decide the best thing to do is silently but directly remedy the situation.

I go up to the counter and order the sausages.

Then, a couple of weeks later, another incident comes along. Needing help after breaking her leg, my friend Tara is staying over, and I've accommodated her in the room that was my grandma's. As soon as I move Tara in, I can immediately detect Grandma's presence in there as well. Sensing her sitting poised and cross-legged in the chair, I perceive that she is miffed about what she considers an invasion of her space. Even though she thoroughly enjoyed being around Tara while she was alive, I get the strong impression that she is not happy at all about having company in "her room."

My hunch is quickly confirmed by back-to-back questions from Grandma: "What's she doing here? When is she leaving?"

I'm taken aback by her bluntness, but I am just as baffled as to how to handle what is happening given that Tara is right in front of me. Figuring out how to navigate between two worlds isn't a problem I've ever been faced with. Lady Aberlin always possessed the skill to quickly and gracefully traverse between the real world and the Neighborhood of Make-Believe whenever necessary, but I only feel dumbfounded and inept.

I hesitate to say anything until Tara blurts out, "Your grandma's here, isn't she?"

"You can tell?" I say, astonished.

"Yes!" Tara says. "I can really feel her here. What's she saying?"

I decide that she probably doesn't want to know all the details of Grandma's disapproval with the arrangement, so I choose my words with care.

"She's asking how long you're staying," I say.

Without reluctance to register any of this as real, Tara dives right in and tries to talk to her on her own.

"Oh, come on, Grandma," she says. "My leg is broken. I just need a place to heal."

I feel the strong sensation of Grandma settling back into her chair, and I tell Tara she seems to have relaxed a little. At least until Tara and I talk about her potential return after another surgery.

"You mean she's coming back?!" I hear Grandma burst out.

Tara and I laugh, but this is the most I can take for one evening.

It's late one night, and I should be in bed. But I just can't let the issue go. My grief counselor's affirmation hasn't been enough to fully sway and convince me. Even reading about how other cultures view the afterlife, often welcoming and honoring episodes like these, doesn't make me a believer.

Tonight, I am compelled to continue searching for and combing through online stories of people who experience talking to and feeling the presence of lost loved ones. The personal accounts depict people easily embracing this, noting familiar statements: *I know they are with me. I know they are watching over me. Death wasn't a final end, just a transition.* Examples of divine, life-saving intervention often follow or just a general sense of knowing they are not alone in the world. I notice that each statement seems to come without any hesitation, doubt or embarrassment. Embracing and believing their experiences seem to come so easily for them. What is getting in the way of me believing my own?

Toward the end, but not yet knowing it was close to the end, I recall Grandma's outlook began to shift. While still keenly insightful, the focus and content of her sayings changed. She seemed to have a constant need to remind me of our bond with one another. She would say things like "Remember I am with you always, regardless of the circumstance."

Once, she remarked to Tara how she was "going to cross the street soon, and Jaye won't be able to come with me this time."

She seemed to know what was unfolding, while also remaining secure in her belief that our connection would endure. Thinking back to this, I find myself wondering why I persist in resisting my own experience. Especially when these occurrences have actually helped provide me with a reprieve, almost like a pause button from grief. Is it possible that these ethereal interludes can be a real part of the process? But my mind quickly dismisses the idea as too far-fetched.

So I continue to question. Stay skeptical. However, this all changes when I come across a series titled *With Open Eyes* on PBS. My body relaxes and an excited thought pops into my head: *If these issues are covered on PBS, it has to be legitimate!* I click on a related article chronicling different reactions to the voices of deceased loved ones. Not just from those who eagerly welcome and believe, but also those who are afraid to acknowledge what they are experiencing due to fear and stigma surrounding the possibility that there may be something seriously wrong with them. As I scroll, I start to better recognize myself both in the stories of what people describe as well as in those who are fearful and push it away.

Not resolved but feeling more assured now that I have PBS on my side, I am able to let in everything I have read enough to give my experiences more weight and make them more believable to myself. In particular, the idea that maybe this was just a transition and not an end. While not completely convinced, I notice I am a little more willing to sit with this idea. At least enough to turn off the computer and finally go to bed.

Month 6

Time does not bring relief; you all have lied . . .

—Edna St. Vincent Millay, "Sonnet II"

I REALLY DON'T KNOW WHERE TO BEGIN or how to explain.

Everything feels wrong as I drift from one unfinished thing to the next. Ungrounded, lost and longing for something to weigh me down. But nothing has the force to hold me still for very long. Even in conversation, I am unable to finish complete sentences, and I will soon stray from whatever it is I mean to say.

13 Months

Right now, in my office, I am leaning back in my chair, lifting my hands to cover my eyes. I'm unable to work productively. My mind bounces between thoughts like a wild, unpredictable ping-pong ball. This has become my new routine: lack of focus and interruptions to my concentration. Scattered in thought, it becomes increasingly clear that even the most routine task now takes me four times as long to accomplish. I question and doubt each detail, rethinking and redoing things which, in the past, I would have automatically and quickly completed.

The paper I am working on is nearly unreadable, all marked up with cross-outs and cross-outs of the initial cross-outs, along with nearly illegible, fully irrelevant notes scattered along the edges. I babble to myself. I go back and forth striking through, then adding, then crossing out, then hastily noting some new strategy to consider. The pressure to complete what I need to finish today mounts as there is not much time left. I make a sharp move to put my head on my desk and try to use harshness to jolt myself into working more efficiently. *You have got to get it together NOW!* I scold myself. I am not sure if I'm surprised or not that this ends up having little effect. Undeterred, I escalate the reprimands, believing that, somehow, this approach will corral me into completing at least something.

Inside, I know that I am a total mess. I grit my teeth just trying to hold it together enough to function each day. But everything is coming apart, and I feel as if I am sinking down into a mass of quicksand. My energy levels plummet, and I notice more and more that I feel tired and depleted even at the beginning of the day.

Wanting to escape what is happening at work, I fantasize an image of myself at home. I daydream that I am laser focused and productive. Engaged with what I need to do over the weekend. I let myself believe this will bring some respite and relief from the internal chaos here. I leave work optimistically clinging to this scenario and striving to convince myself that I am sure to gain some success and peace of mind soon.

But nothing changes. At home on Saturday, I notice little difference and feel equally defeated. I realize this at once, standing in the kitchen looking over a half bucket of water I started filling so I could wash the floor. *When did I start this? What pulled me away?* Then I remember I was doing a load of wash. So, I go downstairs and discover that this too has been forgotten. Worse, I realize that I forgot to put detergent in and will have to start over from the beginning. I drift from one activity to the next, unsatisfied and unsettled. Every idea that pops into my mind is like a shiny new toy enticing me to immediately drop what I am doing, filling me with the hope that each new task will be what I need to make me feel accomplished. Only to discover that I am disillusioned just the same.

In what seems like no time at all, it's 10 p.m. and I'm standing still, eyes glazing over the disarray of my home. Everything in an incomplete state. The bucket of water now cold, a portion of clean but unfolded laundry strewn across the sofa, the new sheets for the bed left half-made since morning and a barely started sewing project I've deluded myself into thinking would take thirty minutes to finish. Now too tired to complete anything, despair sets in around the certainty that I am a complete and utter failure.

Convinced of my own incompetence, my mind seems unable to remember that half-completed or neglected tasks are nothing new. It's just that before I could easily reassure myself that everything would eventually get put in order. I never viewed these situations through the lens of disaster. Now, it's like I have fallen down a tunnel chute, ending up in a funhouse of mirrors, certain that the severely distorted and dire images about myself and my situation are real.

Added to this are thoughts and reminders of Grandma. Thinking back to growing up in her home, I compare myself to how she always appeared to have things under control in any situation. She tried to teach me so much, but what have I done with what I learned?

Grandma's ability to balance the schedule of a military operation with the elegance of a dance kept the house running smoothly under a firm but graceful hand. Not only smoothly, but with the most loving of details. When cooking waffles, pancakes or French toast for breakfast, she insisted on warming up both the butter and the syrup. She thought cold (or even room temperature) syrup ruined the love in her cooking. I remember how she would reach for the tiny pan she used just for this purpose. In those moments, I could barely wait for the small bubbles to form on the edges, the signal that it was ready.

She had a seemingly supernatural ability to make do, work with and transform just about anything. During play time, what I saw as a faded stack of construction paper would magically turn into hand puppets one day and ribbons of paper to create a flower bouquet or homemade placemat the next. When it rained or snowed, she would quickly improvise. Pulling out the jump rope, she'd attach one end to a door knob, and off we'd go. In the kitchen, I watched in wide-eyed wonder as she seemed unruffled by missing ingredients and any unexpected setbacks. Spontaneously concocting a substitute or whipping up a remedy for a not-so-perfect dish in order to salvage a meal.

It was during these moments that I learned quick fixes like combining lemon juice and milk to create a buttermilk substitute, using a stalk of celery as a basting brush or salvaging burnt toast by scraping it with a knife. During the hot summer months, I watched in amazement as she would manipulate the shades and turn the fans in various positions throughout the day to keep the home as cool as possible. In winter, when I would come home from school for lunch, she would rush to take off my mittens and scarf and prop them up in front of the living room baseboard heater to dry. After lunch, as she would help wrap me back up in my winter coat, I always relished the toasty warm feeling on my hands and neck.

And now, remembering her through this lens of precision and meticulousness and seeing myself through the lens of disarray and chaos, it is impossible not to believe with conviction that I don't measure up. Not only did I not get anything done, I chastise myself, now I must clean up these additional half-messes.

Desperate for some sort of refuge from this internal turmoil, I wander into the room I shared with my grandma when she came on the weekends. It is the one room that has been untouched by mess and clutter. I turn on the lamp as I enter; its dim light faintly illuminates the room. I look around. My gaze lands on the pink teddy bear I bought her one Valentine's Day, and I embrace it, slumping down to sit on the floor. Here, in front of me, is the chest where I have stored other mementos, and I reach to open it.

The first thing I see is the book, *The Big Jump And Other Stories*, a tattered fairy-tale salvaged from my childhood. It was my favorite, and Grandma used to read it to me over and over again at bedtime. I pull it out and open it, finding the pages where I decided to turn it into a coloring book. Reading the story again, some relief sets in as I think back and remember being magically lulled under the spell of the benevolent king and into the story's moral that any goal could be accomplished with strong determination and the wisdom to break it down into manageable steps.

Then, just as quickly, the magic spell is broken. My feeling of relief disappears.

But wait a minute, I think. *Isn't this what I've been trying to do with my grief?*

Haven't I been determined? Haven't I set goals to get over loss? Unlike the fairy-tale ending in the *Jump Book*, none of my efforts seem to be working. Everything feels like it is getting worse, not better. So, I sit with the thought that the magic of this fairy tale, which I believed in for so long so long ago, has burst and dissipated into ash—proving to be another act of deception. It's no different from how Mr. Rogers' Neighborhood of Make-Believe blew up in my face all those years ago. But this time, the one person I always relied on to console and comfort me in the face of despair is the one person who can no longer be here for me.

Feeling a strong pain in my stomach as all of this sinks in, I stand up, turn off the lamp and wander back into the land of chaos that has become the rest of my house. At my wits' end, I decide to summon up my adult-style fantasy thinking once again and envision myself magically organized and efficient at work when I return to the office on Monday.

"Jaye, you are becoming mean," Tara scolds me over the phone.

Her words make me recognize that I am not just in shambles with work and home tasks. This disaster extends to people, too.

I am becoming increasingly difficult, to myself and to others. I can see their frustration growing. And I can't blame anyone when they share their frustration with me. I am frustrated with myself.

Apart from a select few, I have been developing an intensifying urge to push everyone away. Either by not responding to phone calls and emails, finding ways to pick fights over nothing or the steady state of being unbearable to be around. Becoming more and more withdrawn in the process.

Tonight, on the phone with Tara, I am not able to fully recall what we have actually been talking about. But I can easily detect from her bewildered tone that I am probably growing belligerent or antagonistic.

I don't say anything. I know she is right, but I feel unable to stop myself. It's like I just want to get rid of anything that might cause me to feel. Especially more pain. So, I needle the emotional cords, anxious to sever them. Everyone's patience is running thin with me, and I start to wonder whether this might actually be my goal.

Oh, and there's more. There's a list. It dominates my thoughts. I have titled it: My Growing List of Worries. While this list may have started with personal concerns about not having done enough for my grandma, it has now taken a turn toward general panic over every elderly person out there. This panic often does not stay contained in my head. It spills over when provoked. Just walking down the street, in a split second, I become hypervigilant at the sight of an older person or what seems to be an elder/caregiver pair. I find myself jumping to the assumption that there is some type of distress occurring, and sometimes I can't stop myself from asking if assistance of some kind is needed. Usually the response I receive is the same question reflected back at me.

Now, as I sit in the waiting area anticipating my grief counseling session, I think more about My List of Worries. It's like one of those Chia Pet things, half-plant and half-sponge; each worry needs just a little bit of water and then they start to grow at lightning speed. These water drops can come in forms as innocuous as a story on Yahoo! News regarding some issue negatively impacting the elderly. Or, as a commercial about assisted living services or a memory care facility. Anything with images of older adults resting comfortably or enjoying themselves in supremely clean, luxury facilities. Being tenderly cared for by a plethora of hands-on staff. Or assisted day and night in their own home. Depicted as if everyone can afford these offerings. As if they are readily available to everyone.

What doesn't get mentioned or advertised is the cost of dementia and elder care. What I saw on TV didn't match the reality I experienced during the time Millie and I were frantically calling and searching for help. As soon as I mentioned our budget and my grandma's needs, the initially cheerful voice on the other end of the phone would be replaced by a curter tone flatly replying, "Sorry, our agency can't help you." Other calls went unreturned or services denied. Likewise, it was often hard to get a straight answer concerning staff-to-resident ratios. The facilities not wanting to fully disclose that they were woefully understaffed and unable to keep up with basic needs such as helping someone get to the bathroom in time.

Now, when I see these commercials or read a story involving care facilities, my worry acts like it has just been drenched in Miracle-Gro and swiftly balloons into its Chia Pet shape.

"What about those other people?" I say to my grief counselor.

"Which people do you mean?" she asks, leaning toward me.

"What happens to them?" I'm not exactly paying attention to her questions.

She listens patiently as I continue to ramble. "I mean, how are the elderly, our elders supposed to survive if no one is there for them? What is going to happen to them? What about the elderly who don't have anyone? Who is going to advocate for them? I understand that pain might be an unavoidable part of the aging process, but does added, unnecessary suffering need to be piled on? Why can't our elders have their basic needs and dignity met?"

I need to stop and take a drink of water.

"Why don't we slow down a little and go over what you just shared?" my grief counselor asks. She attempts to create some coherency out of my prattling.

"Do you think anyone visits them?" I ask. I am unable to soothe myself or find a sense of reassurance as my thinking becomes more catastrophic. I just imagine thousands upon thousands upon thousands of elderly people abandoned and suffering. Alone.

Afterward, as I am walking to my car, I think back to my first counseling session. The one where I so emphatically presented my plan to stay positive. The one that laid out how this grief process would go. Reckoning with the fact that this plan has turned into an utter fiasco, I can't help but view it like a once favorite but now disappointing toy that didn't live up to expectations. One that ends up being discarded and forgotten.

~~~

Later in the month, with my worries and questions still unresolved, I continue my search for answers while talking with Pastor C.

"I don't mean to be disrespectful, but where is God in all of this? I can't imagine Jesus wants our elders to be left alone in distress or, worse yet, suffer some type of abuse in a nursing home. Aren't we supposed to care for people at the end of their life? Aren't we meant to create comfort, ease pain and anxiety during this time? To make sure that someone who is nearing death does not feel scared and alone?"

As she listens to me, I can feel kindness and mercy radiating from her. Swathed in her compassion, I flashback to my first memories of her. When she initially came to the church as an interim pastor, her bright, caring and open-minded nature was infectious. After meeting her for the first time, Grandma was clearly impressed by her personality and noted how much she "sparkled." But Pastor C also never shied away from addressing issues that concerned her. In these moments, she could be equally direct when trying to galvanize the congregation. Blending her conviction in a necessary change with her "love always and in all ways" motto resulted in people feeling inspired to help more often than not. In a short time, her boisterous influence rekindled the spirt of the church. So much so, that, one day, while at an interfaith gathering for spiritual leaders in the community, a pastor from another church commented that her church was "on fire." Jumping to the conclusion that the church was really on fire, she shrieked until someone calmed her down by revealing that they meant it in the metaphorical sense.

Now, as she replies to my emotional outcry, I smile as I recall all of this. Once again, both her warmth and rousing intentions manifest as she offers some pointed anecdotes.

"There was a time I was sitting with a young boy," she says. "He had suffered a lot of mistreatment and he began to talk about where God had been during it all. I found his comment to be wise beyond his years."

Pastor C pauses, and I eagerly await the revelation.

"He told me he knew God sent someone to him, but that they failed to arrive. 'God always sends someone,' he said. 'Sometimes they forget to come, but God never forgets to send them.' "

"So, it's not that Jesus forgets us . . ." I start to say until another consideration interrupts my train of thought. "But there is so much suffering for the most vulnerable. It is hard for me to accept that Jesus is really here when there is only silence."

Pastor C reflects on my feelings of uncertainty before answering me.

"I believe that because the world is so messy, God needs to be messy too. But He is always in the mess with us. When we feel like we have fallen into a hole, as if we are all alone and no one cares, Jesus is actually in that hole too."

I try to digest this as she adds, "I also believe that just as Jesus has soldiers on the ground, so does Satan. And we see evidence of this in the continued swelling of suffering and injustice. So, what we experience is never an absence of God but the reality of a sinister influence in this world."

She reaches out and touches my arm. "Jaye, how are *you* doing?"

It's clear she doesn't want to continue with theoretical discussions. Not quite sure how to answer, I settle on telling her about my low energy, my scattered thinking, the fighting with myself to get it together.

"I thought at some point I would just bounce back. But that is not what is happening. I feel like I'm sinking and don't seem to have energy for anything. I get confused easily. This makes me feel like I am weak and pitying myself. But the reality is that I don't have any energy, yet I continue to struggle."

"Why the fighting with yourself?" she asks.

I hesitate before answering because I am not really sure how to explain. "Well, right now as we talk, I can't accept that I don't have the energy levels I used to have. I tend to believe the worst about myself. That I am being weak. That I'm a failure. Because, with all this worry, I feel like I am not doing enough."

She looks confused, not able to follow my half-sentences and rambling.

I try to clarify. "I don't even recognize myself anymore. I haven't had any energy to volunteer at church or in the community, and I don't like that. I had always imagined that I would be doing more. That I would have so much more to give back. I didn't expect to have such a lack of energy and I feel like I am not contributing or offering anything. I mean, I don't think Jesus meant for us to just get dressed up and sit in a pew for one hour a week. Isn't it more about the service we provide? About what we do the rest of the week? Aren't we supposed to always be out there helping people?"

Her eyes shift upwards as she thinks. Before responding, she touches my arm again. "Well, yes," she says. "The idea is to go out and offer service of some kind. But service comes in many forms. Don't forget the power of prayer. Praying is doing something important. When I send out the list of prayers and concerns, praying for everyone carries great value. So, if you are doing that, never tell yourself that you aren't contributing."

My urge is to dismiss this, to tell her that just having me

pray is going easy on me. Instead, eyeing the idea with suspicion, I probe for deeper understanding. "So, my praying *is* doing something? This *really* counts as a contribution?"

Pastor C nods and offers a very clear example. "What I can tell you is that when I am out on the street late at night doing work for the church, I need those prayers to keep us all safe. In truth, I can feel those prayers. You don't know how much more at ease I feel going out into the night knowing that people are praying."

When she says this, a related memory of my grandma flashes in my mind. She had been part of the church's prayer chain. When a call on the prayer chain came to her, I could always tell because something in the tone of her voice quickly grew focused and serious. She would begin to speak in a hushed whisper and take notes of the prayer request. It was as if an intense stillness descended through the air. A sense of something sacred. I remember, too, that I never questioned whether she was doing something important with those prayer requests. I knew her prayers were a valuable contribution. And, it is in this moment, I feel a distinct shift come over me. With the combination of the memory and the words of Pastor C, my resistance and doubt vanish and I finally believe—really *believe*—that praying is doing something.

At the end of our meeting, she tries to offer me added solace by recommending a book to me. "*God on Mute* might help you regarding your question of silence and if Jesus is really there. It really gets to the heart of grappling with what might feel like unanswered prayers."

Later, at home, I sort through what Pastor C shared, trying to find some more relief. I concentrate first on the idea that Jesus doesn't forget anyone. Even when there is suffering. Even when so many are left alone. This provides me some genuine comfort. But then I question, is it just us humans that are the real problem? The ones causing all of this suffering for each other? Is that it? While Jesus may be with us "in the mess," as Pastor C called it, there wouldn't be this mess of suffering if we hadn't been the ones to create it. Bringing both of these realizations together, despondency sets in as I am unable to unsnarl this dilemma. I give up and go back to feeling that the world is truly as wicked, greedy and frightening as I imagine it to be right now.

Things continue this way until, one night, I try to use the metaphor of grief being like an ocean wave to help me get through my sense of struggle and despair. But the first thing I notice is that it no longer feels like just a wave pulling me under the water. Closing my eyes, I picture water pouring in from everywhere, gushing through the windows and under the doors, shattering each pane of glass and bursting up through the floorboards.

I can't stop it. No longer even an ocean wave, my grief has turned into an all-out cyclone.

Month 7

Don't grieve. Anything you lose comes
round in another form.

—Rumi, "Unmarked Boxes"

MAYBE I *SHOULD* GO.

Many people keep telling me the same thing in different ways.

You need a vacation.
Why don't you go away for a little while?
Take a short trip.
It might give you some perspective.

Even my grief counselor agrees. "I think this would be good for you."

I consider it and decide to go to Mexico. Since I traveled there on a regular basis in the past, it would be the easiest to plan. Settling on a small town that I have visited before, one that is close to the ocean on the Yucatán Peninsula, I notice that I do feel a little relief and even a little excitement. But I'm not there yet.

Before I leave, I notice that my "being mean," as Tara called it, is intensifying. I'm often losing patience quickly and misinterpreting the intentions of others on a regular basis. The growing frequency of these episodes has me imagining myself becoming a type of Jekyll and Hyde. Thinking back to the story, I can't recall if Dr. Jekyll was always able to plan the transformations. Did he control what was happening each and every time? Did he always drink the potion before the change or did it eventually come on unannounced? Was he able to still control it in the end?

I feel as if my changes are becoming more frequent all on their own. Sometimes out of the blue with little or no warning whatsoever. This becomes evident while at the store one evening, picking up some items for my trip. I end up walking down an aisle just staring at the rows in front of me. My mind drifts once again to weighing the decision of whether I should or shouldn't go. I know that I am grateful to even be able to take a vacation, but my mind remains restless. Thoughts keep popping in.

Is this really a good idea?

Why am I doing this?

Isn't planning this trip actually just adding more stress?

Stuck in my head with this cloud of internal uncertainty, I remain unaware of someone standing near me until I am jarred out of my own thinking by a sweet voice.

"Are you okay?"

Looking up, I see a friendly, young store employee with pink streaks in her tousled hair approaching me. Since I am at a store, a reasonable interpretation of her question would be that she could help me find something if needed. Instead, I jump to the conclusion that she is questioning my general well-being and sanity. Fueled by this distorted assumption, I give her a fierce glare, my brow furrowed.

"What's that supposed to mean?" I say sharply. "Do I look like something is wrong?"

Immediately, her friendly smile drops as I see her facial expression change to shock, and I feel utterly horrible about how I have just treated her. Stunned and aghast at my behavior, all I want to do is take back those words. I try to apologize, but it is too late. She quickly turns and leaves.

I stand in the aisle, alone, dismayed and disgusted with myself. If this trip means I will return to being at least semi-decent to others, then I definitely need to go.

The night before my flight, after picking up yet another cheeseburger, I survey my half-packed luggage as I eat. Still questioning whether I am doing the right thing, I can't seem to make a firm choice or be confident in making any decision. My over-analyzing mind fixates on the potential outcomes of going or staying. I fast-forward to each alternate outcome, both of which end in some type of emotional catastrophe. If I go, it's the story of a trip filled with stress and unforeseen problems. If I stay, my mind insists that my grief will only increase.

Consumed with this back and forth, I begin to believe that all choices are destined to be wrong. Added to this is a prevalent sense of shame. These are not real problems, I tell myself. You are incredibly lucky to have the opportunity to go on a vacation. Why do you only think about the worst when you could be thinking about what to be grateful for? As the self-criticism piles on, I move further and further away from being any type of ally to myself. Eventually, less from any decisiveness of my own and more from a sense of inertia, I go.

My eyes are still closed, but I can tell it's morning by the sound of plates shuffling. Then the smell of coffee.

I crawl out of bed and walk down to the breakfast area. Because of how awkward my communication has been, I hope I'm able to sit alone. This turns out not to be as the tiny tables have already filled up with at least one person. I notice a young lady reading her book who looks unintimidating, so I approach her and ask if it's okay to sit with her.

She smiles. "Of course. Please."

As I take in her gentle smile, I feel myself take a deep breath and notice my nervousness begin to subside. It's as if my body is telling me that it is safe to relax around her and just be myself. I learn that her name is Sally. She is here with her friend Meredith, and they are both from Canada. Meredith soon joins us and the sense of comfort and trust I initially felt with Sally quickly expands throughout my body. I find myself able to talk with them both just fine, and I feel an added sense of hopefulness peeking in.

Over the following two days, I welcome a simple routine of enjoying the warm weather and spending a little time each day with Sally and Meredith. But the nights remain challenging. I still find sleeping difficult, and constant nightmares continue to catch me off-guard. In these dreams, my grandma is in some type of distress. Both memories of distress that actually happened and new, imaginary moments storm into my mind each night, and I am unable to reach her. I remain awake after these dreams and wonder why they continue to come so strongly. It is as if my night mind is doubling down, clenched and unwilling to let go. Will they ever stop?

During the relaxation of the day, I notice a stark difference in what my schedule has become. Perhaps unsurprisingly, I find that the frantic urge to command myself into manufacturing and sticking to a new post-caregiver structured itinerary does not consume me in Mexico. And the pervasive worry, badgering self-doubt and inability to stay focused or make decisions seems to be taking its own vacation. I have not told anyone here about my grandma's death or the heavy weight of grief. In fact, it has actually been a relief not to talk about it. My schedule now, lighter and less forced, largely revolves around playing UNO with Sally and Meredith. I feel like I am slowly beginning to catch my breath.

In addition to the regular rounds of UNO, this new relaxed schedule includes a daily check-in concerning any notable news at the inn. Besides Sally and Meredith, there are two others who are staying for more than just one night. There is Liliana, a woman from Argentina, and Tim, an older man from Canada. Tim remains aloof, but Liliana has been chattier; and the brief spurts of conversation with her are very enjoyable.

In observing Liliana and Tim's interactions, Sally, Meredith and I have begun to wonder if they have started a little romance. At first, it was friendly hellos between them each morning, but this has noticeably grown to include flirtatious laughter. We create a "news" segment specific to Liliana and Tim's interactions and check in daily with each other for any breaking developments. It isn't long before the news segment morphs into a soap opera or telenovela unfolding in front of us. Flirtation progresses to lingering glances, then fleeting hand-holding at breakfast, then heightened laughter behind closed doors at the inn. This last stage becomes so pronounced that, one rainy afternoon during UNO, Sally, Meredith and I can't restrain a collective gasp.

The soap opera takes an unexpected dramatic turn one morning when I come down to breakfast and notice that

Tim and Liliana aren't sitting together at the same table as usual; I can feel a pronounced tension in the air. I sit down next to Meredith, and she quickly leans forward, poised to reveal the latest chapter. It appears Tim and Liliana have had a spat. She becomes more animated as she details the argument, complete with waving her arms in the air as Liliana had done before storming off. After breakfast, I see Liliana checking out of her room. I'm sad to see her go.

Though this soap opera has all-too swiftly concluded, Sally, Meredith and I have no trouble finding other things to replace this portion of our day. I find myself really enjoying my time with them, and my relaxation continues to grow. But my schedule is not the only thing that is more relaxed. Each day I find myself more at ease in my own body. My overall breathing has gradually become calmer. My muscles less tense. Maybe this is the start of better times?

One day, while walking into town for some water, we come across a worn-out sign on the side of a shop. It is a series of sentences related to the ocean and a buoy. With some letters or words slightly weathered and others completely gone, it's difficult to determine what is really being said. We come to an agreement that it seems to be a metaphor for navigating life, cautioning us to stay close to home and avoid drifting into danger. I tell them I will ask around and see if our deciphering is accurate.

Later that night, I come down to play UNO and deliver the news. We were off. Way off. The sign was really just instructions for how to mark the ocean with the buoy.

Sally nods her head up and down and reflects. "So, it wasn't as deep as we thought. We were just over-thinking it."

Such a wise lady, this Sally.

Later in the week, Sally asks if I would like to join them for dinner. I say sure, and then Meredith nudges Sally's arm. "Maybe you should let her know about Roberto."

"Oh, yes!" Sally says. "That's a good idea." She goes on to say that it appears the owner of the restaurant might have a little crush on her. She shares that he is really very kind and seems a little lonely. Earlier he had offered to drive them into another town for some sightseeing, but she ended up feeling uncomfortable and called to change the plans.

"I haven't been to the restaurant since then, so I'm not sure what will happen. And sometimes he isn't even there. But, just so you know."

With the sun setting, we walk at a slow pace along the beach to the restaurant. When we enter, I notice Sally offering a small wave to someone. She turns her head slowly to me and mumbles out of the corner of her mouth, "That's him."

After being seated at our table, we order some food; and, just a short time later, Roberto rushes over to sit down with us. He immediately focuses on Sally and repeatedly shares his disappointment over her cancellation of their sightseeing outing.

"I was so looking forward to it. I waited and waited for you."

Sally nods along as he talks and finally manages to interject polite apologies when Roberto briefly stops talking long enough to take a breath. Eventually, she reminds him that she did call and left a message.

"Yes, yes, I know, but I was waiting and waiting for the time to come and so looking forward to seeing you."

Sally develops a puzzled look on her face and calmly responds, "But I'm here now. Why don't you enjoy this moment?"

I feel my breathing falter at these words. I find myself repeating them in my head. I know the essence of her simple statement is not something new or remarkable. What is new is that I find myself paying attention. Not just to the meaning, but to how, like a reflex, she instinctively embraces and lives out her own words.

I can tell I have a lot to learn from her.

After dinner we part ways. I go back to the inn and sit outside watching the ocean. I think more about Sally and, for some time, relate it all to my grief and every other challenging emotion that has surfaced during my grieving.

Maybe it doesn't always have to be such a struggle.

"Jaye! Jaye!"

It is a new day. I gradually come to realize that someone is calling to me. I look up from my table at the local café and am both surprised and happy to see Liliana. She hurries over to me and insists I need to go with her right away.

"Sure," I say, "but where?"

She explains that she is staying somewhere new and has met an incredible woman. "She gives healing treatments. She is the real deal. Trust me."

My eyes rest on Liliana as she shares this, and I feel my heart palpitate a little, though am not sure why.

"Alright, let's go," I tell her. And we're off.

It turns out this woman is only about four blocks away. I'm not sure what I expected but, based on how Liliana presented this as some type of new adventure, I thought it would take longer. Liliana uses a key to open the gate to what looks like a small garden paradise. Lots of trees, bushes and flowers. It is so beautiful.

Liliana asks me to wait at the garden table. I watch a tree branch slowly sway in the breeze. Liliana soon returns and says it looks like everyone is out.

"Everyone?" I ask.

She shares that the woman who does the healing treatments is Alma and the owner of the house is Juanita. There are two additional women here who are renting rooms. Liliana tells me to come back for lunch tomorrow.

"It is okay," she promises. "We all invite guests. Just please come."

The next day, I arrive for lunch as planned. I am a little nervous as I am still not sure if being an unannounced guest is really okay, but my nervousness goes away as Juanita opens the gate, greets me and lets me know they're really looking forward to having me.

She offers a short tour of all the plants and trees flowering in the garden and, while standing under the shade of one, I notice out of the corner of my eye another woman approaching us. Juanita sees her, too, and we both turn in her direction. She walks toward us at an unhurried pace, dressed in a long white skirt, embroidered shirt and sandals with straps that crisscross over the tops of her feet. Her brown wavy hair flows slightly in the breeze.

"Oh good, you're here," Juanita says.

And with that I meet Alma for the first time. Her beaming smile, so wide it causes her eyes to shut slightly and curl at the corners, takes me in immediately. I smile back. She leans forward to give me a welcoming hug. I feel a gentle, genuine warmth from her—it's as if a gust of air has enveloped me. Her hand rests on my arm, causing me to lock eyes with her. Her next smile is accompanied by a slight giggle, and she gestures for me to walk with her toward the dining table outside.

We all share a small lunch feast, followed by dessert and coffee. Over dessert, Alma moves her chair closer to me. Looking directly in my eyes, she offers to give me a treatment. I ask what a treatment entails and find her explanations of clearings and chakra balancing both harmless and appealing. I say sure, and she asks if I would like to come back in about three days. I explain that I will be leaving before then, so Alma offers me a time later that afternoon. She tells me to wear white if possible, and I agree.

As Juanita walks me out, she shares more about Alma.

"Please understand that she doesn't often agree to give treatments so quickly. She only does it when she senses that the person is ready. You will see, she really is a true healer. She was born with a full set of teeth. Do you know what that means?"

I find myself tilting my head a little to the right as I am known to do when trying to figure out what to say. I actually have no idea what being born with a full set of teeth means and pause before sharing my curiosity. My momentary hesitation quickly evaporates in Juanita's warm hug goodbye before she closes the gate.

I know that I don't have a completely white outfit with me, but when I get back to my room, I try to identify something that will work. Standing in the doorway, I consider that this will be one of my last days here. Reflecting on the trip, I am able to register that a genuine sense of peace has developed—it is as if I can almost be a little positive about the future. I bring to mind all that I am taking away from my time with Sally and Meredith and my other experiences here, and I become determined to try and bring the changes in perspective home with me.

I still have several more hours until I return to see Alma, so I start to think about how I need to start packing and planning for my departure. Along with this train of thought, nervousness floods back in. *Am I sure I will make it to the airport in time? Maybe I need to re-check the details? Should I set a second alarm to make sure I don't oversleep? Maybe I should start making a list of everything I need to do when I return?*

Startled by how quickly these worried thoughts cascade in, I feel my breathing become short and shallow. As I stop to take several deep breaths, I know this can only mean one thing: anxiety's abrupt return. Realizing this, I am discouraged at how quickly the nervousness and doubt arrived. A growing sense of dread also makes its return known. It's as if they have orchestrated their re-emergence perfectly and are now lying in wait on the other side of my mind, ready to ambush any lingering peace and determination I feel. More like competitors than companions, and I am their contested territory.

I start to wonder if I have just been kidding myself about all the tranquility and calmness I thought I was embracing. As if everything is actually too good to be true. Fooling myself into believing all this can last. Now, I feel compelled to consider that it might only be a matter of time until the other shoe drops and this peace of mind will fully disintegrate upon my return.

Later that day, I arrive back at the house.

This time Alma is there to open the gate. She smiles and ushers me in. I follow her up a winding staircase to a room filled with crystals and candles. We arrive to the treatment room where I see a massage table off to the left and two chairs placed up against a wall. She leads me toward the chairs and motions for me to sit down.

Standing in front of me, she provides additional details

about what will take place during the session. I ask a few questions, and Alma patiently addresses each one. As I listen to her, I initially feel a sense of calm; however, as her eyes continue darting off to one side, I soon get the impression that something is preoccupying her attention.

When she speaks again, I'm startled to hear her blurt out an apology. She is distracted by a petite woman, she says, who is dancing beside her.

Alma begins to mimic dance steps, tapping her feet side-to-side. She explains that the woman is moving in this way. Also, she is adamant that she has things to say. "She is small but very forceful. I don't think she is going to go away."

I pull back from Alma in shock, unable to speak. I feel paralyzed.

"Do you know someone like this?"

It could only be Grandma, and I tell Alma as much.

"Okay," Alma replies. "She is very persistent and says that she has a lot to tell you."

Imagine that, I think. *My grandma has a lot to say!*

Alma starts to deliver a rapid series of sentences. So fast, they seem to fall on top of one another. "She wants you to know she is happy and healthy, and she is at peace. She also wants you to stop beating yourself up. There is no need to suffer. She knows you loved her and did your best in taking care of her."

I nod my head but continue to sit in silence, unsure how to take it all in.

Alma sits down in the chair beside me. She leans toward

me to share more. I start to wonder if Alma can sense my uncertainty about what is happening because she becomes more emphatic that I listen to my grandma. Tapping the tips of her fingers into the palm of her other hand, Alma emphasizes everything my grandma is saying.

"She insists that you need to listen to her. She knows that you are hurting, and she wants you to release yourself from the pain you are causing yourself. There is no reason for you to be sad. She is happy, and she is still with you."

Alma goes on a little while longer with these messages, indicating once again how my grandma continues to dance as she talks. But before long, Alma stops. She tells me the woman has left. Turning toward the massage table, she asks me to get onto the table to begin the treatment session.

Still in shock, I find it difficult to follow her instructions and am only able to make stiff mechanical movements. Somehow I manage to climb onto the table, where I try to concentrate on what Alma is saying and doing; but my mind is distracted and whirling in disbelief from all that just happened.

What was THAT? Can I really believe any of this? I mean, wasn't the information just kind of general? Shouldn't I be much more skeptical?

Not willing to trust my own perception of this experience I start to wonder if anyone would believe me if I told them, as if external confirmation is the only way I can give myself permission to believe. *Maybe I should just keep it to myself. No one is going to believe me anyway, will they?* I tell myself to stop with the distracting questions and try to stay focused on the healing treatment. My mind calms a little, but I still find it gravitating toward questions and disbelief. Finally, I rest on what I can't ignore. That what just happened *felt* real. To me. Maybe I need to get to a point where that is all that matters.

As if reinforcing this reflection, I cannot deny that what Alma shared had a tremendous impact. I genuinely feel better, more at peace. The heaviness of grief seems to have lifted somewhat. Isn't that a gift in itself? Didn't this confirm what I had been thinking months before about my relationship with Grandma? That it had not actually ended but merely transitioned and transformed into something new?

As the treatment allows my body to settle, my mind starts to release itself from the rush of questions. The healing session continues and lulls me into a deeper state of relaxation. Feeling more grounded in my body through the combination of remedies Alma has used, I sense about an hour has gone by.

Nearing the end of the treatment, Alma reports that my grandma has returned once more with a final message. I tense up, expecting additional wisdom to be unveiled when Alma reveals her actual words.

"She wants you to stop eating so many cheeseburgers. They're not healthy for you."

And with that, the treatment comes to an end.

Month 8

You say your mind's made up, but I wonder if
resolution alone is enough. . . . Things
don't always go smoothly.

—Higuchi Ichiyō, *Encounters on a Dark Night*

BY THE GLARE OF THE COMPUTER SCREEN, I stare at a no-frills image of an aqua blue, vintage rotary phone resting on the bottom tier of a sparse wooden shelf. The simplistic image has such a strong hold over me that I can't stop looking at it. I envision the room just as bare. Orderly and peaceful. That nothing complicated ever happens there. It is 2 a.m. and I have been back from Mexico for several weeks. With the return of some of grief's greatest hits, such as interrupted sleep and anxiety, I decide I have no choice but to get up and take charge. With the peacefulness I found in Mexico rapidly slipping away, I search online for ways to try to salvage what is left of it. This is too important to lose. I am not going down without a fight.

I start with what I can replicate from my trip and zero in on creating a calmer, more simplistic home environment. Plugging this intention into Google, I am surprised by the vast number of websites that come up, all with one thing in common. The word *minimalist*. Browsing through some of them, I am startled to discover that this trend extends far beyond my initial thought of redecorating my living room. It appears that there is a whole minimalist movement out there.

Scrolling through the website, I have this eerie sense that it holds some sort of key for my situation. I just don't know exactly what that is yet. I spend the next two hours reading through posts and take several things away. One, I am not the only person overly bothered by old emails piling up in my inbox. Two, there is actually a lot I can do to shift my lifestyle around if I choose to take that jump. And three, one of the guys from the website appears to use a lot of hair products and the other is enthusiastic about sandwiches.

The peace and calm from my trip began to evaporate immediately upon landing. Since my connecting flight was cancelled due to an ice storm, I searched for an alternative route home the same night. However, I arrived at an unfamiliar gate and became disoriented in the airport. Feeling frustration surge up my throat, I decided I couldn't figure anything out until I finished passing through customs, but this intention was quickly thwarted by long lines and delays.

Finally clearing customs, I realized there was still a chance to catch a bus home. I wanted to sprint to ensure a ticket but suddenly realized that I was both starving and in need of a restroom. I prioritized the restroom, believing that I was sure to find food once I got to the bus terminal. This turned out to be true . . . sort of. The only food available was a small stand with pizza, hot dogs, muffins and beverages. Above the stand, in red handwritten bold letters, a sign read: CASH ONLY.

Uh oh, I thought. All I had in cash was $5 and the equivalent of $20 in pesos. In this deserted area of the airport, there were no ATMs or money exchanges. I hoped desperately that the cashier was willing to work with me.

"Absolutely not," she said, shaking her head wildly enough to send her earrings waving back and forth.

"Okay," I tried to bargain, "I understand your point that the pesos can't count as cash, but could I interest you in a trade? I will give you all of my pesos which equals about $20 in exchange for just $10 from you."

If successful, this exchange would result in enough money for a pizza.

"How . . . about . . . NO!" she shouted back, clearly annoyed.

I decided it was best to discontinue my short-lived bartering career. As I climbed the steps to the bus for the long ride home, my only relief was that I was at least able to afford something to drink.

"Well, how was your trip?" my grief counselor asks at this month's session.

"I do feel better," I share. I give her a summary of the main events and positive emotional shifts.

When I get to the part about the treatment session, she gasps. "This really was a healing time for you," she says.

I muster a courteous smile while nodding politely in agreement. I rein myself in by deliberately saying little more about the treatment and consciously leaving out that the skeptic in me has already started tearing down this experience. Dissecting each moment and finding ways to question, doubt and discredit all that occurred. Having successfully reduced the other part of me—the one that still holds onto the heartfelt memory and believes in the truth of what happened—into a fading presence, the skeptical part won't let up on the indoctrination that none of it was real. Insisting that grief doesn't work like that. It's as if allowing in the full force of the treatment experience would amount to letting myself off the hook too easily.

Intentionally trying to shift the focus away from any more talk of Alma, I start talking about my general efforts to maintain the peacefulness I found. How desperate I am to keep this calm focus despite my mind's tendency to revert to the frightening places.

"What I can say is that I feel like I've found a clue to the path I need to take. It feels right keeping things simple and slow. I'm just unsure of where this path goes. It still feels like I am walking in the dark . . . but, maybe that's okay."

At work the following week, I remember to try asking myself: How can I keep things simple? Resisting an urge to spiral off into many directions, I focus on what is really my top priority. Only then do I move on to the next task, and then the next. Working this way, I am able to increase my focus and reduce my mental wandering. I notice an inner sense of calm begin to surface. I take this as an indication that I am on the right track. At the end of the day, as I turn off the light and close the door, I can honestly tell myself I made some progress.

Given that it is still early for me on this path, I need to remember these more centered times. The confusion, distraction and sense of dread that have come hand-in-hand with grief still seem poised and ready to surge up from below at any moment. And many times, they do, whirling me into anxiety and self-doubt, sucking me back into the belief that everything I am doing is wrong and that nothing could possibly turn out right. Panic sets in, and I frantically grasp for the compulsion to create overcomplicated plans and to-do lists. As if caught in an undertow, I become disoriented and lost as I'm carried away from my inner certainty of simplicity and calm. Instead, I succumb to a conviction that I need to keep moving. None of it is kind and compassionate, though. More like a warning foretelling me that the menacing presence lurking from the start is still fast on my heels. This lingering sense of dread, gnawing at me since Mexico, continues to loom over any attempts at optimism. Deep down, something tells me that this isn't over yet.

Month 9

As love is union, it knows no extremes of distance.

—Sor Juana Inés de la Cruz

"I'm going to do this," I announce to Tara one night after work.

"Woohoo!" she cheers me on.

"Besides, who is really going to know?" I explain. "I never say anything out loud when I am in public."

"I can't wait to hear what happens," she says.

What I've decided to do is honor my grandma's birthday

by going all out. For this event, I am aspiring to cast aside my doubt and skepticism even if only temporarily. Instead, I am going to try to trust and fully embrace her presence that I feel is still with me. Birthdays were a big deal to my grandma, and not just her own. She loved to make a glorious event of anyone's special day even if it was just for an hour or two. Known to bring out her best dishes, deck the dining room table with her daintiest linen tablecloth and bake the guest of honor's favorite cake or cupcakes, I would not have been surprised if a circus or fireworks suddenly appeared during one of these festivities. Because of this, I want to plan something that would do her justice and spend some time in her old neighborhood, doing things she loved.

During my counseling session, I detail the planning I have done over the month with my grief counselor.

"Going out to lunch is a must," I share.

"Of course!"

From there, I list the other crucial elements: strawberry cupcakes with buttercream frosting, balloons, *Lawrence Welk* and pink roses. The things my grandma loved.

Later that day, I run through the list one more time with Alejandro.

While nodding his head in agreement he suddenly interjects, "You might want to try and get those apple fritters she always liked. I know the bakery is all the way across town—and they sell out of them quickly—but she never stopped talking about those doughnuts."

"Great point!" I say, and quickly add *Try and get the*

doughnuts to my list.

When the big day finally arrives, after securing several apple fritters, I meet Millie for lunch. We settle into a table at one of Grandma's favorite restaurants and spend time reminiscing.

"What are your favorite memories of Grandma?" I ask.

"There are so many," she says. "But my favorites always revolve around her cooking and all the care and affection she put into it. Whenever there were family gatherings and celebrations, many didn't realize how she would get up at 3 a.m., sometimes earlier, to get preparations underway. She knew her cooking made people feel loved and brought the family together, and she took the planning very seriously. I'll always remember the way she used to pull out *The Settlement Cookbook*, carefully taking off the rubber bands, which were the only things holding it together after so much use. She would re-read all the recipes and handwritten notes attentively, as if for the first time, even though she had everything memorized. She scrutinized each recipe to ensure everything would come out just right." She turns the question back on me. "What about for you?"

I decide to share one of my all-time favorites.

In her 70s, shortly after my grandfather's passing, Grandma expressed a strong desire to take driving lessons. Being able to drive was a passionate goal she had been unable to complete until now because, for some reason, my grandpa had not been too keen on the idea. After enrolling in a private driver's education course, she talked to me and many family members about her driving lessons and how she had successfully passed the written test that granted her a learner's permit. None of us doubted the authenticity of her achievement.

The first time she offered to show off her driving skills, I didn't think twice about hopping in the car. Things seemed to be off to a good start as she adjusted the mirrors, pulled out of the driveway efficiently and successfully stopped at the corner stop sign. But it was all downhill from there. As she turned onto a semi-busy street, she showed no interest in picking a lane and seemed quite content to drive very much under the speed limit. As horns started blaring, I quickly grasped that the reality of her driving abilities did not match at all with the stories she had been telling. As it dawned on me that this might have been the reason for my grandpa's objection all those years ago, I felt my heart rate spike. I honestly feared for my life.

"Pull over! Pull over!" I shouted and pleaded with her to let me take the wheel. Panting as I switched into the driver's seat, I noticed her visible annoyance. She looked straight at me and said, "Well, gee, I was only getting warmed up." To which I didn't hesitate with my blunt response: "Grandma, there is no getting warmed up on National Avenue."

Neither of us can stop laughing as we continue to recall many more memories like this. Unbeknownst to anyone else, Grandma sits at the table with us, laughing along. Still believing I need to conceal these experiences, I don't say a word about it.

Later, after lunch is finished, I venture to one of her favorite shopping malls. Walking past the little storefronts, I am clearly aware of her strolling along with me. A few moments later, I feel a gentle tug on my arm. Turning to look, I am not at all surprised to see an old school candy shop.

As another way to honor her day, I decide to buy a box of chocolates. Browsing the smaller boxes, I hear her exclaim, "No, the big one. Up above!" I look up and immediately know which one she wants by its flaming pink and yellow decorations. I hesitate only slightly. Who does she think is going to eat all of these? With the apple fritters, extravagant lunch, cupcakes and now chocolate, I wonder if I am going to get through this celebration without needing to buy a larger pair of pants.

At the end of the day, I take notice of how embracing her presence instead of fighting with myself over the logic of it has left me feeling joy and happiness. In this moment, grief doesn't seem so harsh. I can perceive a movement to something different. Almost as if, living this way, grief is not really my enemy. From one of my grandma's favorite *Lawrence Welk* episodes, I hear Nat King Cole's "L-O-V-E" playing in the background. Singing along, I take a commemorative photo of the balloons, pink rose bouquet and chocolate placed in front of my grandma's rocker.

This is a really good day. Encouraged by my ability to embrace her presence, and filled with sparks of weightless ease, I continue to sing Lawrence Welk's tunes to myself as I

13 Months

get ready for bed. I fall asleep clinging to this sense of lightness and joy, hoping it can stay.

Month 10

To get lost is to learn the way.

—Swahili Proverb

What keeps pulling me back here?

My mind flashes back and fixates, drifting to the final days, hours and moments of my grandma's life. These memories play out like black and white film on an old, clunky projector. Most of the images whirl by, but some of them stall until the make-believe movie projector resets itself, tugging the next one forward. In these moments, I feel physically frozen. What is it that keeps pulling me back here?

With my fists clenched, eyes closed and every muscle in my body tense, the question doesn't necessarily need an answer; it's more a plea for release.

Not able to withstand the emotional pain that always accompanies these memories, my instinct is to do anything I can to ward them off, as if I am a villager arming myself with garlic and a cross in hopes of repelling Dracula. But my feeble attempts are doomed from the start; I have no power over what feels like some unnatural force dragging the images to the surface.

All of the flashbacks center on one specific theme.
MORPHINE.

At the beginning of her decline, I knew what this word meant, but I wasn't prepared for all it would entail. A difficult issue for anyone to navigate, morphine also seemed to evoke very rigid and inflexible opinions. Once the morphine was initiated, an avalanche of differing advice and instructions came my way. Each as emphatic as the next.

They just want to over-sedate people.

Don't do that. She still might get better.

Don't you know that this means it's the beginning of the end?

People don't really feel any pain at this point anyway.

You're taking her voice away.

The last one always felt like a dagger to my heart. Take her voice away? Are you kidding me? I only wanted to fight for her, advocate for her. Follow what she wanted me to do. But what this might be became hard to determine as her verbal skills faded.

I began frantically turning to hospice staff to help me learn how to communicate with her in this new phase. Using all the support and information that they provided, I made every effort to adapt and find new ways to understand and listen to her. But more obstacles developed as other voices continued to chime in or badger me about what I should be doing differently. With all this extra noise, I needed to uncover a quiet spot for myself just to pray and beg for guidance. So much so that I became desperate to find an escape.

"Where are you right now?" my grief counselor asks.

It takes her words to yank me back from this flashback tunnel and remind me of where I really am. In her office.

"I fell back into it," I respond.

Half of me is now with her, and half is still focused on what have become nightmarish reruns. I try to return fully to the present.

"I just can't seem to shake them," I explain. "And I don't know why *these* specific memories keep popping up or what it is that pulls me back. I get so confused because just when I think I am moving forward, feeling better or have turned a corner with grief, these memories seem to pop up out of nowhere. I can quickly plunge into a deep and murky place. One where I go back to ruminating on and chastising myself for every decision I made. Convincing myself again that I did everything wrong. I don't know. . . maybe because it's not just the memories that haunt me, but also the additional weight I felt forced to carry from the many opinions, criticisms and judgments thrown at me? I remember feeling ganged up on during moments when I was at my most vulnerable and most in need of support and understanding. I felt kicked and punched in the stomach. Why did some people have to be so mean?"

During her time with me, so much remained unpredictable. On the weekends especially, it was always uncertain how the time, particularly the nights, would go. Sometimes she would sleep soundly, needing my assistance only to use the bathroom. Other times, she would be fraught with nightmares and would scream out in distress while punching her tiny fists at something only she could see. Waking abruptly, I would quickly try and enter her world to better understand what she was seeing so that I could reorient her to the present. Holding and rocking her to assure her that she was safe. Transitioning into her world and doing my best to see what was behind the curtain of dementia was also necessary when her sleep became disrupted and time would get turned around. She often called me "mama" instead of my name, and there were so many times I would need to figure out what era she was in or what she was gazing at in the empty corner of the room, so that I could determine what she needed.

Sleep deprivation, worry, stress and a hypervigilance

regarding her needs began to escalate. All of this gradually became the norm. Still, I stayed grateful as I knew her symptoms and situation could be so much worse. Others had to contend with personality changes or aggressive behaviors. Sometimes to such an extreme that it felt as if the person they were now taking care of was a stranger. Everything I was going through was business as usual for any caregiver in my situation. Even with the mounting stress and distress, I always considered myself one of the lucky ones.

And then, as her health and memory further declined, more significant changes started to appear. She kept losing weight no matter how much she ate. Visits to the ER, followed by short hospital stays became more frequent. Things were not looking good and, after one such episode, our doctor discussed the need for hospice services. While initially an emotionally challenging adjustment, the much-needed end-of-life care that she was given and the support I received became a huge solace for both of us. After the approval for hospice services, she was assigned a treatment team. From then on, I maintained ongoing contact with Lena the RN, Bella the CNA and other providers as needed.

Next came a series of falls. However, my grandma always seemed to bounce back. Until one time, she didn't.

The last fall started out the same as the others. The usual process was that I would receive a call from hospice letting me know what had happened and if any medical intervention was needed. I would then talk to her or go see her, and she would usually be in a cheery mood, listing off things she needed.

At first, with this fall, she seemed to be rebounding again. One night, before I left the care facility, we shared our usual bedtime routine, saying, "God bless you, angels keep you and remember Jesus is with you."

I walked out the door, promising I would be back first thing in the morning, and she blew me a kiss good night. The next day I optimistically opened the door to her room, anticipating her sunshine-filled smile. Instead, what I was greeted by brought me shock and disbelief. Before me sat a hollow, silent version of the grandma I had known.

Unable and unwilling to accept this, I turned to find Neecy, one of the kind-hearted staff at the facility, coming in through the door. She motioned me with her hand to join her in the hallway. Still in shock, I tried to take in all that she was saying. Something had changed dramatically. My grandma had gone from smiling and able to converse—all signs that she was rebounding—to withdrawn and non-communicative. This change coming out of nowhere and no one knowing exactly what happened or why.

The only possible incident they could pinpoint was that a new bed, the hospital type, had been delivered. And that when they started to transition her into it, she had become ornery. Perhaps this small disturbance created a larger impact than expected. Despondent and emotionally unable to listen anymore to what Neecy was trying to tell me, I tried to stay present but couldn't. Fragments of sentences started to linger in the air.

"Lena from hospice is here. Do you want to talk to her?" Neecy asked. She sounded encouraging.

In a daze, I walked out to find Lena on the sofa in the entryway. I sat down beside her. Questions began pouring out of me.

"What could have happened?" I said, shaking my head back and forth in desperation. "I don't understand. I was here just last night. She showed the usual signs of rebounding. What is going on?"

Lena, listening quietly and compassionately, waited for me to finish. As tears streamed down my face, I felt her gently touch my arm. Slowly, she began to respond to my questions.

Those final weeks felt as if I had found myself in the midst of an unforecasted, rapidly growing blizzard. One where you are caught woefully unprepared. Where you register far too late that this initially light and innocent snowfall has quickly transformed into something so thick and so fast that you can no longer see anything beyond what's directly in front of you. Soon it becomes impossible to keep your eyes open because the storm has now morphed into sleet, beating down on your face. With it, the wind picking up and whipping like knives cutting into your skin. Still, out of a sense of survival, you try to find your way enough to keep going.

First, you shield yourself by closing your eyes. You try to cover your face with your arm. But this offers little protection against the pellets of ice bombarding you from every direction. You find it impossible to walk in a straight line because now the harsh wind has begun to blow directly into you. It is more ferocious than anything you've ever felt, more merciless than you ever thought nature could be. You have become so disoriented that you no longer know if you are on the right path. So terribly lost you might as well be going in circles.

Then, just as suddenly, the blizzard stops. It's over. You slowly open your eyes to survey what is before you. You're waist deep in snow, wondering if there is any way to move forward from here.

After the counseling session, I continue to find myself lured back into this tunnel, replaying Lena's response that all signs indicated my grandma's deteriorating condition. And then gently providing me with what options were available to keep her as comfortable as possible. When I am deep in this tunnel, my old, now familiar habit of making demands on myself likes to come along for the ride. Barking orders to stop allowing myself to get pulled back here and then scolding me when I am unable to stop. One particular night, on the edge of tumbling fast down the hole, my mind manages to grab onto something Grandma tried to tell me in Mexico: *Don't be so hard on yourself.*

Does this count? I want to ask her. Is it okay to lighten up on myself with these specific memories? I want to go back to the same old question: *What keeps pulling me back here?* But I know if I react to the question in the same old way, nothing will change. As uncomfortable as it feels, this time I think of my grandma's words to help me ease up on myself and take a risk with something different. While the question remains the same, I manage to ask it with less resistance and self-scolding. Instead, I make the effort toward a more tender, more curious approach. This time, I ask with a willingness to discover the answer. *What keeps pulling me back here?*

With only this subtle change in tone and intention, I notice my body relax slightly, and I get the sense that there is something more for me to discover. More than the painful memories I have been enduring with clenched fists. I finally feel like there might be some sort of meaning to be found in this question. With another attempt at kindness, I ask again.

What keeps pulling me back here?

The answer to my question does not come right away, but it does come.

Month 11

Stop calling yourself damaged. How about saying that you are "recovering," "healing" or "working on yourself."

—Horacio Jones, *I Am The Love Of My Life*

I'M AT DINNER WITH MY FRIEND REINA, in a packed jungle-themed restaurant, to celebrate some stranger's birthday. I've only come to visit for the weekend, and I remain extremely uncomfortable and blind-sided sitting at the table with fifteen of Reina's friends who I am meeting for the first time.

Someone blurts out, "Deactivate my FaceBook account? That's social suicide."

I sit quietly, listening to several of the guests argue back and forth about the pros and cons of social media, trying to put the pieces together as to how I actually ended up here. Just twenty minutes ago, Reina picked me up from the airport. She sprung it on me in the car that we would be going to a birthday dinner party right away. Knowing her all too well, I suspect she had hatched this plan a while ago.

"Why didn't you warn me?"

"Because I know how shy you are," she replied matter-of-factly. "You would have tried to get out of it. This way it's a surprise."

"And I don't have a choice?"

"Right," she said. "Besides, we're here now and I strongly encourage you to go with the flow. End of discussion."

A little bit about Reina and me. People regularly ask with an air of confusion how we are friends. Reina, with her boundless energy, inability to stay settled for more than seven minutes at a time and fearlessness in the face of any new adventure; and me, with my typical energy level just a step above a nap, capacity to stay settled for more than seven hours at a time and the need to research and investigate every detail before agreeing to a new adventure. On the surface, we seem like a misfit pair, but we fit well because we balance each other out.

Reina is the person who has challenged me the most to get out of my comfort zone. Always in a loving way, but

Diary of a Caregiver's Grief

usually not gentle. More like someone who, while watching you take small steps to get acclimated to the water in a swimming pool, determines you need to take bigger steps and sneaks up behind to push you in. Over the years, I have learned the hard way to give in to whatever she is challenging me to do. When Reina strings together the words "I strongly encourage you to . . .," she may as well be the Godfather making me an offer I can't refuse. She is not the sort of person you can say no to for very long.

Back at the dinner party, wanting me to engage more, Reina jubilantly exposes to everyone that I have zero social media. This ends up being a big deal. The FaceBook guy gasps and several others ask me how I communicate. No longer able to just sit quietly to myself, I glare at Reina as she mischievously begins to giggle.

The next morning, while drinking coffee at her kitchen table and thinking about last night, I ask her pointedly, "Why do you always get so much joy out of making me uncomfortable?"

"It's not about making you uncomfortable," she counters. "I just know that it is good for you—for anyone—to try something new at least once in a while. If you don't like it then you can stop. But at least you can tell yourself that you tried it."

I absolutely hate it when she is right. Not wanting to reveal that I am giving into her logic so quickly, I hold back from saying anything more right away. But she can see it on my face.

"I'm glad you agree," Reina smiles proudly. Then her facial expression shifts into something intensely serious, as if she is already onto the next thing she sees needs challenging in me. She takes the magazine in her hand and smacks it on the table. "And remember, Spanish today!" she shouts like a drill sergeant. "No more English!"

Everything Reina is saying makes me think back to this month's counseling session. I had asked my grief counselor about how life changes with grief and if people eventually go back to their normal routine.

"It really is different for everyone," she responded. "Some people find it impossible to return to their past life and need to learn how to construct new routines."

As we talked more about it, she frequently emphasized that it is really important to pay attention to oneself during the process.

"The key here is to really listen to what feels right and not force yourself into something that doesn't work for you. Even if you hear that an activity works for a lot of other people, it is completely okay if you don't like it."

I considered her explanation in light of what I'd been up to months ago. When I was adamantly forcing myself to follow a self-prescribed plan of what I thought I should be doing, without allowing myself the opportunity to decide if what I was doing felt right. No wonder it made me more miserable.

Still drinking coffee, Reina asks about our plans for today.

"Well," I say, showing her a photo from a magazine, "I saw this ad for ziplining and I've never done that before. What do you think?"

She looks at me, then the picture and then back to me again. "Are you sure this is what you really want to do?"

As Reina is calling and booking us for the next session (just two hours from now), I think, *Well, what's the big deal?* All I see in the ad is a woman smiling with lush greenery all around her.

"This was not a good idea!" I whisper frantically.

We are no longer at Reina's kitchen table drinking coffee. Instead, we are walking up the extremely tall staircase leading to the first jump. I am taking short, frequent breaths. The palms of my hands are covered in sweat.

"In the picture, they didn't show how high it was," I say. "I just saw the smiling lady and all the green trees."

Reina can't stop laughing, and she doesn't look back. "Where did you think we would be flying from?" she says. "The ground?"

Given that I am not at all fond of heights, I try to find the humor in the fact that I left out such a critical detail when imagining what ziplining would entail. "I was trying to be more spontaneous and didn't think too much about it. I just focused on the picture and thought it would be fun."

We're part of a tour group, and it is too late to turn back

now. I watch as Reina steps onto the landing, telling the instructor that she is fine and doesn't need any assistance. With one small push, she is off. As I step up next, I quickly grab onto the instructor's shoulder, not wanting to let go. I feel it is best to inform him that I am not at all like my friend.

"It's okay," he says, "I'll give you a count of three. Will that help?"

When he goes from *one* to *two*, I try to stop him. "How about a count of six?"

But it's too late. He says *three* and I am pushed out of the nest.

※

The night before I leave, I do a little work in Reina's kitchen to prepare for the upcoming week. Something I am working on creates a spark in my mind: What I've been struggling with isn't just about the grief process anymore. There is a curious sense that I have gone through all these feelings before with my PTSD (Post-Traumatic Stress Disorder).

I can't believe I didn't make this connection earlier, and something tells me to do a search linking PTSD with caregiving and grief. What comes up takes me completely by surprise. An article titled: *For Some Caregivers, the Trauma Lingers*.

Devouring the information, I feel an overwhelming sense of relief. It is as if the article has supplied me with a critical clue into the blind spots of what I have been going through. And with this clue, I'm able to rip away the curtain to my grief for the first time and illuminate what lies behind it. There is a logical explanation for what has felt like an unending struggle. I am hungry for more. I discover a few other articles and websites related to caregiving, memory issues and hospice services, all of which allude to a condition known as post-caregiver PTSD. It is not uncommon for caregivers to experience trauma symptoms once the caregiving is done.

"Reina, can you come here?" I holler. "Read this and tell me what you think."

"Wow! This makes so much sense," she assures me. She sits down next to me to read more and starts shouting out the points she thinks are most important for me to remember. All while simultaneously filing her immaculately manicured nails. We both agree that this is a big piece of the puzzle in understanding what is happening with me.

With tremendous relief and a growing sense of validation, I now know why these specific and upsetting memories, negative thoughts and nightmares keep popping up. It isn't that I've been making things up or been weak in my grieving. There is a genuine and legitimate reason based on shared experience for my fixation on certain things and my inability to let them go. I finally have an answer to the "what keeps pulling me back here" question.

But now that I understand what keeps bringing me back, the bigger question is what am I going to do with this information? I know that simply learning about post-caregiver

PTSD is not going to help me by itself. I need to choose to use this knowledge to help deal with my grief. Without taking that leap, I will continue to stay stuck.

So, while relieved, I also know that digging into this will take more work and effort. Part of me doesn't want to undertake this as the past months alone have been hard enough. Finding this new information makes me feel like I have been running a marathon, but that now, unexpectedly, another hill that I need to tackle has popped up in front of me. Part of me would rather just stop running, give up the marathon and look for the nearest ice cream stand.

As Reina drives me to the airport the following morning, we laugh about the adventures from the weekend. Especially the ziplining.

"That turned out to be a lot of fun," I say.

"Once we got to the kiddie levels at the end you seemed to calm down," she agrees, "and even started to leap off the landings on your own."

Once again, she is right.

"Well," I say, "small steps still count!"

As she pulls up to the airport drop off point, my mind returns to the discovery that I have a new task to face in addition to my lingering grief. Will I choose to use what I have discovered to help myself cope?

While I would love for it to be Reina's responsibility to challenge me once again and push me up this hill, the unavoidable truth is that the only one responsible for this is me.

Month 12

The important thing is not to think much
but to love much.

—Santa Teresa de Ávila

A THICK ENVELOPE ARRIVES in the mail from hospice. The one-page letter includes an acknowledgement of the fast approaching one-year anniversary of my grandma's passing. Also mentioned is the upcoming conclusion to the thirteen months of counseling support, with a recognition that the grief process doesn't neatly wrap itself up after one year. The remainder of the contents consists of their newsletter featuring ways to cope with an anniversary date, as well as a list of support services that can continue after the thirteen months come to a close.

At our session last month, my grief counselor brought up the upcoming anniversary date, both because of its significance and also because she would be out of the office.

"I would be more than happy to schedule you with another counselor if you like," she thoughtfully offered.

I responded after some careful consideration. "I think I'd like to try a month without a session. I'd like to see what happens, if that is okay?"

Now, looking over the packet of papers, I notice I don't feel an emotional pull in any obvious direction. I spend the next few days somewhat suspended. Almost like I am holding my breath, waiting to see what happens on the first anniversary of Grandma's death.

When the anniversary date finally arrives, I get up and decide to walk outside. Still noticing that I don't feel anything of significance, I suddenly hear Grandma whisper in my ear.

"The word of the day is *ha-cha-cha!*"

I can't help but smile. My intuition gives me a clue that my grandma doesn't want this day to be a morbid one filled with gloominess. Resting on that, I hear more from her.

"Don't remember me like this," she goes on. "Think of me full of life, doing all that we did together."

Tears well up in my eyes. "Of course, Grandma," I whisper.

I also have the strong sense that she wants me to go out

and get a piece of pie in her honor.

"You got it, kid, you got it!"

Throughout the month, more memories of my grandma glide in and out. This time they span a variety of different time periods and are filled mostly with the joy, tenderness and fun we shared. I think back to growing up as her tiny, constant companion in the kitchen. Spying on whatever treats she was preparing, during the cold winter months with my back against the stove to warm myself and in summers sitting on a chair by the kitchen table with my legs tucked under me. She would carefully measure out the ingredients for cookie dough, then laugh and stroke my hair when I carelessly threw in as many chocolate chips as I could. We were always at odds when it came to putting the dough on baking sheets. She wanted to use as much of the dough as possible for actual cookies, but I was more interested in eating as much of the dough that I could get my hands on right away. To redirect my attention in order to finish baking, all she had to do was run outside and turn on the water sprinkler.

Then there are memories of all the fun times while she was under my care. Times when we decorated Easter eggs, relishing the chance to continue a tradition we had done together since my childhood. Or hummed along during the free Sunday music concerts at the botanical gardens and took "walks" under the trees where I would wheel her up and down the sidewalks. The many breakfasts at Espuma where, afterward, we would visit the craft store for her to pick out a new bracelet or flower clip for her hair. Times filled with joy, not distress or worry.

My mind weaves back to childhood nights of lying in bed, still able to see her sitting in her chair in the living room through a crack in the door. She rocks steadily by a soft light, mending socks, folding laundry, watching TV or listening to music. I would always drift to sleep with such a deep sense of love and safety.

I find myself often reflecting on who she was as a person and where her deep faith in a loving, kind Jesus came from. Outside of the home, the church was the other place you could regularly find my grandma. She eagerly wore many hats there, from Sunday school teacher, to member of a women's circle, to quilting group, to several planning committees. I often wondered how her faith persevered through the Great Depression, two World Wars and the multiple personal traumas, challenges and mistakes she confided in me. After what she had endured, I wondered how her heart remained so open and free of bitterness, far more so than I suspected mine probably would. This was a question I had asked her many times, and it always led her to delve into the mistakes she had made in her life and what she learned from them.

"Honey," she would say, "I am not perfect. Far from it. So how can I expect others to be? Besides, that is not what is expected of us. I just try to do my best, which is what the Lord asks us to do."

It was from this place that she offered lessons rooted in her faith that would leave a strong imprint on me. Messages of seeing the best in others and putting one's faith into action.

Time and time again, I saw her make an effort to live the lessons she taught me. Watching her see the best in others and put her faith into action left a strong impression. Nearly every morning, she would carve out time to sit and read a daily devotional. One day, when I asked what she was reading, she responded without looking up from her book.

"Worship isn't just for Sunday. I don't like to leave the Lord out of any day."

She was never one to close the door on someone in need or to shame and judge them. She remarked that in times when she was suffering and in need there had always been someone to extend a hand to her, and she wanted to give back what she had received.

However, there was one lesson where we remained at odds: forgiveness. Whenever this topic came up over the years, we struggled to see eye to eye. My grandma insisted on unconditional forgiveness while I expressed serious doubts that it was the emotionally safe thing to do in every situation. She based her idealism on all the times when forgiveness had successfully set things right. My skepticism could not ignore the occasions where I or someone I knew had been willing to open the door to forgiveness only to be cruelly tricked and harmed once again.

Added to my doubt were times when this lesson appeared shrouded in contradiction. Especially when it related to a family member. In these cases, any glaring double standard or questionable motives were intentionally ignored or abruptly brushed aside.

These discussions eventually intensified into clashes, and we tended to stay entrenched in our opposing positions as if behind official battle lines. Whether knowingly or not, both of us strategically drew attention to the factors that bolstered our view while carefully excluding any details that might contradict or conflict with it.

Her points were unchanging and familiar. Forgiveness was always the right thing to do. We should always show compassion and mercy to others. Without forgiveness, inner peace and security were not possible.

And the questions I posed were equally predictable: "Grandma, does forgiveness mean that you just let someone walk over you again and again? Does forgiveness mean that you let yourself open up old wounds? Doesn't there sometimes reach a point where things are just too late? Where someone has to accept the consequences of their choices?"

These were the moments where I outright resisted the guidance she was trying to offer me. My heart already hardened by hurt and anger, I remained adamant that I couldn't let down my guard and that boundaries were vital to protecting myself. Sensing she was trying to be patient with me, I also detected some exasperation in her voice at her simple reply.

"Honey, that's no way to live. We can't expect to be forgiven ourselves if we don't forgive someone else. We are all human and make mistakes."

Yet, even with my uncertainty, I couldn't deny the fact that she seemed to be at peace in her life and that this peace seemed to come from her own acts of forgiveness and her conviction in its power. I had witnessed her forgiving others time and time again. Usually it was offered without requiring any discussion on what had created the conflict or any apologies from the person who I felt was in the wrong. Her unflinching ease baffled me. I found myself filled with doubt and confusion. Did she just want to avoid conflict? Not hold someone accountable? Disregard the complexity of the situation in favor of a simplified remedy? But Grandma denied all of this. Instead, she always indicated her desire to embrace forgiveness and undermine resentment. Certain that forgiveness made her more centered in herself. Stronger, not weaker.

And the times when I summoned up the courage to do as she did, I couldn't deny the way that the images I had crafted, and the stubborn certainty of what I thought I knew about a situation or a person, suddenly shattered. The storylines I had manufactured in my own mind turned out not to be accurate reflections of reality. I often sat frozen, taking in the stark difference between what I was so sure of and what actually stood in front of me. It would dawn on me that all the pain, grudges and resentment I had carried for so long with such self-righteous indignation had just ended up causing more pain for myself and everyone involved.

It was these experiences that finally ushered in a more

far-reaching understanding of the lesson she was trying to teach me. That, all along, it wasn't just about forgiveness. Forgiveness was merely the result. The deep faith in and ease with which my grandma offered forgiveness came from living her life with a heart filled with love versus one filled with bitterness, anger or hate. It wasn't true at all that she didn't create boundaries for herself. It was just that she established hers from a foundation of love which she insisted provided the most safety and protection. For her, forgiveness for someone never came at the expense of neglecting or not loving herself.

In contrast, living with a heart full of anger only limited and blinded me. While it's true that not all the acts of forgiveness ended up with a storybook ending, my form of emotional protection was like pouring salt in my own wounds. Yes, hurt and betrayals persisted. But using anger and fear instead of love to create boundaries only encaged me, fueling more hurt and bitterness until it was all I could see. Eventually I realized that it wasn't just about the act of forgiveness, but how forgiveness needed to come from a place of love. This would ultimately prove to me the deeper element of the timeless, often repeated part of this lesson: Forgiveness frees the forgiver just as much.

While our wrangles with forgiveness never neatly resolved themselves and it remained the lesson I most struggled to fully embrace, I sense another purpose in the reflection. I now find myself in a place where I am called to act as both the forgiver and the one being forgiven. I feel as if

Grandma is provoking these memories to direct me toward an even more difficult layer of the lesson, that of forgiving myself. Without the forgiveness foundation she managed to establish in me, I wonder if self-forgiveness would even be possible now.

I have been treating myself with just as much anger and resentment as I have dished out to others in the past. And none of it feels good. I still obsess over ways I let her down, the times I didn't do enough. When I consider forgiving myself, it feels like letting myself off the hook.

But the truth is that she worked with me on this lesson, too. And she seemed to want to emphasize it to me during our final months together. One afternoon, expressing remorse about a time in the past where I felt I had let her down, she waved her hand while sitting in her rocker.

"You proved yourself a long time ago, Jaye."

And then, more mystically, nearing what I didn't know were going to be her final hours, she found a way to communicate her love to me long after she had ceased speaking. If I had truly made such a mess of things, why would she be relaying this to me in her last hours?

More and more often, reminders of the complexity of who she was in life shine through, along with the lessons she tried to live and show me again and again, and memories of lightness and joy. The recollections of distress and sadness slowly start to diminish. While the distress is far from gone, I can honestly sense a significant shift in my focus, and along with this shift comes a strong message.

13 Months

It is time for me to heal and to accept who I have been throughout this whole process. It is time to find a way out of the tunnel I keep falling into. It is time to find the way back home and back to myself.

The real experience is less like a gigantic shift and more like a tiny stir. I begin to perceive this message more and more over the month as the negative thoughts and self-criticism seem to lose some of their fierce power and grip. I delve into finding more information on post-caregiver PTSD. I go back to the original articles and websites. I read and re-read them. From there, I find other websites such as the Caregiver Space and the Alzheimer Journey. I am more and more relieved, validated and empowered to know that my experiences are real, and that I am not alone.

As much as possible, I need to put all this information into action. First, I make a decision to increase my grief supports. I make a plan to check in with my doctor to restart acupuncture sessions. I also go to the clinic website and scroll through the list of holistic services offered. I learn more about the benefits of naturopathic medicine, meditation, tai chi, aromatherapy and Reiki, and I consider each option.

Along with this, I focus on the intrusive negative thoughts I regularly experience. Now I realize that those powerful flashbacks around morphine were no fluke. They were the start of releasing myself from a hex of self-doubt and self-condemnation. No longer hypnotized, I comprehend that my eagerness to devour all of these negative self-messages without question has been like succumbing to false advertising or propaganda. With this information, I am convinced that I have found another way. One where I can take baby steps in this healing process.

I know that I will need to learn a new and kinder approach to dealing with these unrelenting negative thoughts. Whenever I am able to catch and recognize them, instead of immediately falling under their spell, I try to be curious about and actually think through them. I accept them, but also slowly start the process of dismantling the thoughts and recognizing they can be transformed. From there, I work on mustering up the courage to ask myself if I want to continue to believe their message or choose another meaning and storyline.

Peeking through like the sun in an expanse of dark clouds, I am conscious of my growing potential to think and believe something different.

Month 13

Be yourself; everyone else is already taken.

—Oscar Wilde

"Well here it is! I can't believe thirteen months have gone by already."

It is my last session, but I have done little to prepare for it. While sitting in the waiting area, I decide I just want to see where things go. And that's exactly what I tell my grief counselor. Once the session begins, I find myself having a hard time focusing. My mind starts to go astray with thoughts of what I need to pick up at the grocery store and other errands. These don't necessarily feel like distractions. More like I'm ready to be somewhere else.

She brings up the anniversary. I fill her in on what happened and how I felt that day.

"I don't think it's going to be a day that I remember each year," I say. "I'll be celebrating dates like her birthday. That will be far more significant."

My grief counselor nods in support of what I have decided works for me.

Well before the end of the session, I run out of things to say as my mind continues to wander. This isn't at all how I expected my final session to go. Feeling anti-climactic at the closure to all these months, I ask my grief counselor if there is something more I should be feeling or doing.

"What were you expecting?" she says.

After the session, I can't decide if this end feels more like something is unresolved or the start of something new. Although, I'm not even sure what that "something new" might be. What is clear to me, however, is that at the start of these thirteen months, I had unknowingly created a specific expectation for myself. An expectation that some definitive transformation from grief would occur by month thirteen— a transformation that would combine getting back to my "old self" but with a clearly noticeable metamorphosis mixed in. All of this would be revealed to me in some sort of dramatic unveiling, complete with balloons and streamers and lots and lots of glitter flying everywhere. I would be waving my arms around with a sense of accomplishment and relief.

But that hasn't happened at all.

"Stop there," Tara interjects. Tara, Alejandro and I are sitting outside having dinner. As I try to explain all of these feelings, Tara disagrees with my portrayal. She says, "None of this means there hasn't been any change. For one, you are definitely a lot calmer now and freak out a lot less. Wait, that didn't come out right. Let me rephrase . . ."

I peer over the rim of my sunglasses and smile.

"No, I get it, Tara. There were a lot of freak outs. I really want to thank you for hanging in there with me. I certainly know it hasn't been easy."

Agreeing with Tara's perspective, Alejandro chimes in, "Before, you often seemed distracted and lost in thought. As if you were somewhere else. You smile and laugh a lot more now."

Then, seeing an opening to revisit the number of Spurs' games we still have recorded, he asks, "Do you think you're ready to delete some of those games?"

"Not a chance," I quickly reply.

So, I guess Tara and Alejandro are right. While there hasn't been any remarkable, glamorous transformation like something on a before-and-after makeover show, I can sense a definite difference. An awareness of things being, well, in process. But from there, I find myself struggling. I'm unable to put my finger on what exactly is different, and I can't shake the urge to articulate what I'm feeling more concretely. A compulsion to wrap everything up into some sort of nicely defined conclusion. Is this urge coming from a desperation for validation? And if so, validation for what?

One night, I find myself back under the conviction that nothing has changed. I wake up from a particularly haunting nightmare of my grandma in distress. I'm unable to reach her. Walking to the kitchen for a drink of water, all I can feel is defeat. *See,* I think, looking out into the midnight sky from the kitchen window, *nothing is different. Nothing is resolved. I'm just fooling myself to think otherwise.*

But instead of getting sucked in, I encourage myself to think over what has really changed. Sure, on the surface things aren't tidy and resolved. Most days, I still struggle with the awkward moments and challenges that grief can bring. Okay, so if none of that is different—what is? And what I recognize is that the real changes haven't been external. It's not the circumstances; it's my perception of them. It's how I deal with things like the nightmares when they resurface.

When looking at it this way, yes, change has occurred. It's just not the change I expected. All this time I've been hoping for something more superficial in nature; but what I've received is more internal and foundational—something that's still brewing and marinating under the surface. I start to wonder if this far subtler change might actually be a good thing, even if it feels a little disappointing, because setting myself up to believe in the unrealistic expectation of a grand transformation has made me feel like I've been holding my breath all month waiting for it to happen. Which is just way too much pressure.

Being aware of all of this does not trigger the release of falling balloons or descending glitter either. But it does bring a sense of relief.

Days later, while cleaning out my closet, I shake out a jacket and a card falls out and flutters to the floor. Without thinking, I reach down to pick it up and quickly notice my grandma's name written out in bold letters at the top. It's a reminder card for an old dentist appointment. I feel as if I've been sucker-punched. Dropping the jacket, I reach for the closet door for support. But it's too late. A hard lump forms in my throat. Tears begin their cascade. I stagger out of the room and make my way toward the living room couch and try to regroup. That's when it dawns on me. Of course I have been compelled to create some validation during this month. A confirmation that all this pain, confusion and inner turmoil has some worth—that meaning and growth can really come out of all of this grief.

Recognizing this, I decide to make a list. Something I can use to remind me of the changes and what I am taking away from this whole experience. A list to help me revive when future sucker-punches occur. One that provides solace in the time to come when I struggle to accept that the combined stress from caregiving and grief took too much of a toll, and that my "old self" would not be returning.

This list is very different to the list I made for my first counseling session. It's not something I've written down, and it's more of a mental collection of things I have come to value and trust. Lessons I want to embrace and continue working on. Gone are the impersonal, callous and prescribed dictates about "getting myself in line" when grief continues to come in waves. All rooted in self-denial and self-deprivation. In their place are items that actually nourish me with healing benefits and have personal meaning based on my first-hand experience. Ones where I am able to think or do something different, even when things are in disarray or uncomfortable.

But here's the thing. None of the items on the list are earth-shattering. Most of them have been said before in some way or another and are lessons I have at least partially learned before. But that's just it; I never went beyond grasping them as abstract concepts. I might have already known these lessons, but they weren't anything I felt fully or absorbed emotionally. Without spurring myself toward emotional insight, I only ever stayed in my head and never started the process of embodying their truth. This deeper feeling and comprehension changed everything, opening up the potential to finally learn how to live them.

First, grief is not, and never has been, my enemy. Nor is any other emotion. This concept makes its way to me via the book *The Wisdom of No Escape* by American Buddhist nun Pema Chödrön. One night, reading a chapter about challenging emotions, I find the words: "If you throw out the neurosis, you throw out the wisdom."

The sentence hits like a bolt of lightning, and I can't stop re-reading it. As I take a moment to consider grief as an ally instead of an adversary, I feel something click in my head, much like getting the last number in a combination before the lock releases.

Because of my training as a therapist it might seem like I should have been better at navigating my experience with grief. What I know now is that, regardless of my profession, the challenging and uncharted waters allowed me to grow in ways I was not even aware that I needed. And my growth experience included some messy times. Very messy. There were moments I felt incredibly lost and everything seemed upside down, moments where it felt like nothing would get better. The inescapable truth is that everything I experienced with grief led me to where I am now.

From the very beginning, grief was my ally. Grief served as a catalyst for shedding the idea that there are good and bad emotions. For ripping away the facade that somehow being happy is "better" or makes me a "stronger" person than feeling uncomfortable, isolated, anxious or depressed. While I spent a lot of time adamant that I needed to be a vigilant warrior against grief, what actually happened when I clung to the misperception of good and bad emotions was far more destructive. I ended up at war with myself.

I recall so many times feeling like a pathetic loser any time grief wouldn't just go away. When messages of *Get it together, Stop wallowing, Don't be so weak; be stronger* filled my head, I always encountered a strong desire to "prettify" what I was really feeling, so as not to irritate or make others uncomfortable. I wanted so much to masquerade as someone other than myself, desperately wishing I could handle grief with the elegance and grace I imagined Lady Aberlin would possess. Maintaining an air of regality, even during the toughest moments. Instead, I felt like a bull in a china shop—clumsy, awkward and graceless. Deeply ashamed and mortified by what was unfolding, instead of honoring what I was feeling and just letting the emotions flow naturally, I desperately wanted to cage myself. But trying so hard to repress and get rid of any emotions I thought I shouldn't or didn't want to have only caused them to get stuck and morph into something truly harmful.

Until I allowed myself to release them.

The problem was never grief or any other emotion. Problems only emerged when I tried to deny and run. There are still many days when an emotion comes up and my knee-jerk reaction is to reject, resist and suppress it. As if quickly drawing my sword to force it into submission and change it. Except, the compulsion to change just becomes another cloak for shame with its underlying message that what you are feeling is bad or wrong and must be eliminated. With this mindset, the only thing I end up pointing the sword at and doing battle with is myself, and there can be no positive outcome from that kind of stance.

But there are other times when I am able to befriend the challenging emotion instead of wanting to change it. Replacing resistance with an awareness that I am feeling this way for a reason and that this reason is important to know. Grief has taught me that when I drop the sword, and instead accept and pay attention to whatever discomfort I am feeling, I learn much more and open the door to growth and transformation.

We can't avoid the dirt. We need the dirt to make new life flourish. It's a part of the path and process and not something to be jumped over or eliminated. Enormous wisdom and value hides in the soil and, without it, we miss out on keys to awareness and healing.

Another lesson is facing the fact that I'm the only one who can give myself permission to determine and voice what matters to me. No one else can do this for me, nor should they. Pulling back the curtain of grief to receive what lay behind it put me on the path to healing and helped me gather my beliefs and core convictions about caregiving and grief.

One: What actually counts as caregiving and being a caregiver? My belief now is that anyone who takes part in any aspect of caregiving, in any way, for any amount of time is a legitimate caregiver. Creating a hierarchy of who is and isn't a caregiver promotes the illusion that there are specific standards everyone needs to meet before "claiming" this title. Did you have help from other family members or friends? Then you are out. Did you have the financial resources to reduce stress for yourself and offer more options to your loved one? I guess you are out too. Were you a caregiver for only a month? A year? Out. Was someone else doing the direct caregiving while you planned, organized and visited?

Definitely out.

These shifting and revolving criteria amount to cruelly and unjustly excluding others, when what we really need is to be supportive. There is no doubt that having friends and family who can help with errands or provide respite breaks significantly reduces the stress of caregiving. And the pressure alleviated by having the financial means to consider services such as 24/7 in-home care cannot be understated. Many caregivers do not have access to these kinds of luxuries. The disparities in care options based on financial resources and other vital factors definitely need to be brought to light so a more truthful discussion pertaining to the realities of caregiving can occur, allowing for increasingly humane and dignified treatment of the elderly. Still, this doesn't delegitimize, in any way, the pain that comes with witnessing the deterioration of someone you love. As caregivers, we need to stick together, to validate each other's experiences even when they might differ from our own. To understand that everyone is struggling and everyone needs kindness. That we have an obligation to help support each other. You know, all that good stuff from Mr. Rogers.

So, I choose to believe in another way, one that honors each unique and individual experience of caregiving. There will always be critical voices. There will always be those trying to determine who is and is not "legitimate." I won't be adding my voice to this chorus of naysayers.

A second belief is in the importance of honoring the personal stories of grief. It gets suggested that grief isn't talked about, but that hasn't been my experience. The issue is not that grief isn't talked about—it is. The issue is that the experiences and stories of grief aren't listened to enough. Personal accounts of grief can be found everywhere. There are grief websites and blogs, filled with people wanting to share their experience, various support groups offered and bookshelves and art displays packed with intimate stories. There is no shortage of people wanting to talk about their grief. It's more that when the topic comes up, especially in small social settings, it is frequently diverted or shunned.

Many, if not most of us, find grief very difficult to listen to. What is it that gets in the way and makes it so challenging to take in? I get a sense that the difficulty in listening to stories of grief is less often about a listener's coldness or indifference and more about feeling overwhelmed, unable to bear the pain in the stories and an uncertainty about how to help the person grieving. Stories of grief are incredibly tough stuff to hear. They bring up feelings of powerlessness, generate fear about one's own vulnerability and yank away any false assurance that we may be somehow immune to devastating loss. How could we be anything other than overwhelmed when listening?

Although, maybe it's not just about the listening itself, but also the expectation and pressure we put on ourselves to be impeccable listeners. To always know just the right thing to say. A significant amount of anxiety can come from thinking we need to orchestrate magnanimous displays of support. We can impose inner turmoil and distress from putting it upon ourselves to find a solution to the person's suffering.

I often felt people's anxiety and agitation during my grief. I have also been in that very same position. I know the desire to quickly turn away or flee any discussion on grief. Feeling terrified, ill-equipped or filled with self-doubt that I have nothing soothing or helpful to offer.

While this reaction came up a lot over these thirteen months, I also experienced another type of response—something I can only describe as a calm listening. With Tara and Reina, there didn't seem to be any internal pressure or anxiety to know just the right things to say or do. In fact, many times, there were few words spoken at all. I had the sense that they weren't plagued with self-doubt, thinking that what they were offering as listeners wasn't enough. Instead, I could feel their listening coming from an inner self-assurance and trust that they just wanted me to know I wasn't alone.

I wonder if listening to grief would be less scary if anxious and distressed listening were replaced with calm listening. Something that benefits not only the person grieving but the listener as well. Allowing all of us to start from an inner trust that we want to do the best we can and have something inherently valuable to offer as listeners. To believe the best in ourselves instead of feeling anxious and filling ourselves with self-doubt about our capacity to listen. Then we could allow our natural, simple and heart-inspired expressions of listening to emerge. No eloquent phrases or grand gestures needed. Just bearing witness as listeners, assuring the person in the throes of grief that we are right there with them.

And, after all of this, as the dust continues to settle, where do I go from here? Grief, combined with ending my role as a caregiver, threw me so far off-kilter that I became entirely disconnected from myself. It was as if I'd abandoned myself when I needed myself the most. I had no idea who I was anymore. Shattered and vulnerable, I became certain that I was a charlatan and a fraud. A fraud as someone with "real" grief. A fraud as a caregiver. Someone who didn't belong.

Along with this, a deep sense of lack took hold. I felt that I was somehow inherently damaged, deficient in value or not enough. This created an inner emptiness that prevented me from accepting, believing in or trusting myself. So, I conned myself into thinking that the cure-all for grief could only be found somewhere on the outside. I certainly couldn't be trusted to know what I needed, right? Without any faith in myself, I started grasping on to whatever trends were being promoted at the time, abiding by them to tell me what to do and how to grieve. I hoped this would also somehow fill the void inside and eliminate my feeling of being a fraud. But when inner fulfillment never materialized, the disconnection from and inability to believe in myself only worsened. Instead of questioning my self-imposed scam, I would move mindlessly on to the next trend, convinced that surely this would do the trick. And the next after that—often in complete contradiction to what I was following before.

It was only when I stumbled upon the information

about post-caregiver PTSD that the tide began to turn. This sparked the thought that there was nothing wrong with me to begin with and raised the idea that I could actually ask myself what I needed in order to heal. More, that I could actually treat myself compassionately as I healed. Once I made the shift from seeking outside myself to compassionately searching within, the sense of lack and view of myself as a fraud slowly started to fade. Making it possible for me to start believing in myself as I move forward. In the end, turning inward and summoning up one's own self-acceptance, appreciation and trust are the only things that can protect us from the lie that we are not enough and don't belong.

Still, there continue to be times when self-doubt, fear or the return of grief's waves surge up far beyond what I feel I can handle. There is no getting away from life circumstances that are messy, uncertain, devastating or all of these at once. I have no fairy-tale ending to offer here. How much time we have is unknown, and loss is certain. I am left wondering if one can really be prepared for grief. I am also more apt to believe that, more often than not, deep anguish during grief is unavoidable and forcing premature "cheeriness" on anyone only compounds that agony. Maybe the best we can hope for is to find some type of relief. One that provides comfort for each unique circumstance and delivers some respite during the despair of grief. Relief that opens a path to healing. Now, when fear and sorrow become all too consuming, I call on back-up support for help. It is during these challenging moments that I grasp onto a specific inspirational saying my grandma always relied on and urged me to use: Let my faith be bigger than my fear.

Over and over, I witnessed Grandma using her faith to deal with life's losses and fears. After my grandpa died, she did just that and used her faith in herself and her spirituality to pick herself back up, keep going and embrace life. Instead of being discouraged when things didn't go her way, she found the ability to laugh (either at the situation or herself) along the way. During this time, she regularly sought out new approaches to enjoying life and creating purpose in her life, even when obstacles stood in front of her.

Now it's my turn. I need to try to find my way after loss just as my grandma did. With all these changes and lessons, I aim to let each day unfold and just keep going. With no final destination or end point in mind, I hope to take in everything I can while trying not to resist or push out what might initially seem uncomfortable or scary. Living this way feels so much better than the frenetic taunting and chastising I engaged in for so long. There is an undeniable spark of lightness, peace and joy when I focus on making an effort to get back up, as my grandma did, and keep on going.

Which brings me back to the predicament of what to do about my grandma's presence. This all comes out into the open one summer morning as I am walking, peach muffin in hand, toward an outdoor table at Espuma, the café we frequently went to for breakfast. Attempting to take the muffin out of its wrapper, I miss noticing a dog's leash tied to one of the patio chair legs. Clumsily, I trip over it, losing control of the muffin. It drops to the ground directly in front of the dog, who swiftly gobbles it up, completely ignoring me in the process.

Wrapper still in hand, I feel a mischievous sense of suspicion about how quickly all of this just went down. As the dog inhales the last remaining crumbs, I wonder if this could have been a well-orchestrated setup.

And that's when I hear it. Grandma's undeniable laughter. But instead of greeting the sound with skepticism or feeling compelled to keep my experience under wraps as I have done time and time again over these past months, I begin to laugh right along with her.

"Well, isn't that something, Grandma?" I reply out loud, for anyone to hear.

Conscious of her presence beside me, I return to the counter to get another muffin. I am now at the point where I want to fully welcome and embrace my experience with her, even if I still can't explain any of it. I know she remains firmly by my side, acting like the combination of a guardian angel and trusty co-pilot and reminding me to live with love.

Keeping this conviction close to my heart, I just continue to go.

Acknowledgments

I would like to express my heartfelt gratitude and love to my friends and family (especially Alejandro) who have showered me with help, patience, understanding, love and a million other things I can't do without. I am at a loss on how to fully describe my deep gratitude here and just hope that my ongoing impromptu outbursts of love and thankfulness do a better job at expressing my appreciation.

I would also like to thank the many people who helped me during times of caregiving, grieving and the writing process.

Those who helped me cope:

All the memory care, hospital and hospice staff who provided countless hours of care, support and guidance. I will never forget all you gave to my grandma and me during such a vulnerable time. I only hope that I can do my best in paying it forward.

The music of Edyie Gormé y Los Panchos, Dean Martin and Armando Christian Pérez (aka Pitbull, aka Mr. 305, aka Mr. Worldwide). Thank you for providing comfort, lifting my spirits and helping me find courage and strength when I thought I had none.

Those who helped me heal:

To the many healers I have been so fortunate to meet. Thank you for your dedication to healing and willingness to share your gifts with those in need. It is only with your collective wisdom and remedies that I have been able to find the path home to myself.

Pastor C and my grief counselor who personify compassion and understanding. Your ability to sit with those in pain, listen patiently and provide comfort is a recipe for healing that I wish for everyone.

The San Antonio Spurs. While watching you season after season never resulted in me learning how to dribble or shoot a basketball, you continue to show what it looks like to keep going when things get difficult, how to get back up after defeat and the importance of advocating for others.

Those who helped me write:

LMM & JV who seemed to mystically appear during the times when I needed courage and inspiration to move forward.

The staff at the neighborhood coffee shop (especially M & D). Thank you for fueling me with creative caffeine concoctions and also sharing your witty, talented and one-of-a-kind personalities. I can't wait for the time when I am able to say: "I knew them when . . ."

LW & MT who took the time to read the early manuscripts, often many times, and give valuable feedback. I am so appreciative and owe you both so much!

Deep appreciation to Horacio Jones, for his generosity in granting permission to quote his work.

Elizabeth McIvor, whose quick-fired and discerning insight during the proofreading process were vital to completing this book.

The angel, KSA, who provided me with invaluable support, encouragement and skillful writing guidance. More, during the many times when I thought I was going to start pulling my hair out from frustration, pulled me back from the brink and helped me continue moving forward. Thank you for your angelic presence during the writing of this book and in my life.

Jane Ryder at Ryder Author Resources who swooped in offering superb resources and extremely hands-on, personable and masterful book shepherding services. More, for your vast warm-heartedness, unflappable understanding and cut-to-the-chase directives that reoriented me when I kept running in circles or fell into a hole.

And especially, Joshua Wagner, a writing mentor and editor extraordinaire without whom I would have been lost. Without your mentoring and open acceptance of me from the start, all the scraps of paper would have never formed into this memoir. I am incredibly grateful for all that you have taught and given me as it led to a truly life changing adventure. While you often replied: "that's my job" to each thank you, it's not what you do—it's how you do it. With encouragement, patience, blunt honesty ("Redundant!"; "What are you trying to say here!"), finesse and wisdom. You are not only a brilliant editor, but also an incredibly gracious and kind human being. I am so lucky to know you.

Thank you so much for reading *13 Months: Diary of a Caregiver's Grief*. If you're moved to leave an honest review wherever you prefer to review books, I'd greatly appreciate it. If not, that's fine too.

If you have your own stories about caregiving or coping with loss, you can find me at https://boook.link/13-months. I'd love to hear from you!

www.ingramcontent.com/pod-product-compliance
Lightning Source LLC
Chambersburg PA
CBHW031250290426
44109CB00012B/511